A PILGRIM'S BOOK
OF PRAYERS

A PILGRIM'S BOOK OF PRAYERS

BY

GILBERT SHAW

A. R. MOWBRAY & Co. LIMITED
LONDON AND OXFORD
MOREHOUSE-GORHAM CO.
NEW YORK

First published, 1945
Fifth impression, 1949

PRINTED IN GREAT BRITAIN BY
A. R. MOWBRAY & CO. LIMITED, LONDON AND OXFORD
9615

PREFACE

A SUBSTANTIAL portion of this book originally appeared as a series of booklets under the general title 'Burgh Booklets.' They were intended to help those who were seeking forms of words to express the prayers of the heart and will, as well as of the head, and by way of affective acts as well as by considered and discursive meditation. As they have been long out of print, it seemed desirable that at least the prayers, if not the introductions to the several pamphlets, should appear again in more permanent form. To them I have added similar exercises and provided a general introduction. It is not necessary to study the latter before using the book. Indeed, it may be of more use to readers when they have become conversant with some of the prayers. A few notes appear at the end of the book so as not to interrupt the text of the devotions. Some of these draw attention to the sources of the ideas or words used, but for the most part I must leave it to the users to recognize my debt to the past when they find well-worn phrases or echoes of the voices of those who have gone before, and in whose footsteps we are endeavouring to follow.

I have to thank the Church Union for their permission to incorporate, under my own name, *A Pilgrim's Meed of Prayer and Praise*, first published by the Society of SS. Peter and Paul in 1924; also Messrs. Mowbray for leave to reprint some original prayers used to preface translations from the medieval English in *Prayers and Meditations for the Lovers of Jesus* published in 1927; and the Association for Promoting Retreats for allowing me to use phrases and prayers from various pamphlets compiled for them between 1928 and 1932.

GILBERT SHAW

December, 1944
S. ANNE'S CHURCH HOUSE
    SOHO, W.I.

CONTENTS

CHAP.		PAGE
	PREFACE	5
	INTRODUCTION	9
I.	A DEDICATION TO THE BLESSED TRINITY	25
II.	A PILGRIM'S MEED OF PRAYER AND PRAISE	36
III.	CREATURE AND CREATOR	51
IV.	AN EXERCISE FROM THE PSALMS	61
V.	A PILGRIM'S PRAYER TO JESUS	66
VI.	THE PATTERN OF THE MASTER	77
VII.	TO CALVARY	91
VIII.	FELLOWSHIP IN SUFFERING	101
IX.	AFFECTIVE REPETITION	129
	NOTES	145

A PILGRIM'S BOOK OF PRAYERS

INTRODUCTION

THIS is a book of affective prayers. Its purpose is to provide material for people who find it a help to have ready-made devotions of an affective nature. They are not intended to be slavishly used. The hope of the compiler is that they will serve both to encourage and guide users to formulate their own prayers, and through them to learn, by use rather than by instruction, what affective prayer really is.

It is not a book about affective prayer. Those who desire to make a study of the detailed methods and the theory may refer to the chapter on affective prayer in the Reverend Francis Harton's book, *Elements of the Spiritual Life*.[1] He comments on the need for suitable material by saying, 'As souls advance they are able to make their own acts, but the difficulty for a beginner is that there are so few books of prayers which can give him any help.'[2] This is a book for beginners.

THE NATURE OF AFFECTIVE PRAYER

A great many writers dismiss affective prayer in a somewhat cursory manner as being that kind of prayer which lies between the prayer of meditation and contemplative prayer. For example, Father Lallemant of the Society of Jesus (*d.* 1635) defines it very neatly in a few sentences, between a detailed treatment of meditation and contemplation, as follows:

'In the second kind of prayer, which is called affective, we give ourselves more to affections of the will than to considerations of the understanding. We consider a mystery, a passage of Scripture; for instance, the words *Verbum caro factum est*. On these we make acts of faith, hope, and charity, admiration, thanksgiving, etc. We take one of God's perfections, as his wisdom, his goodness, his holiness. We consider how it was communicated

[1] S.P.C.K., 1932.   [2] p. 255.

to Jesus Christ and the Blessed Virgin, to the angels, to some saint; we praise God for it; we ask for a participation of it, and dwell as much as we can on the affection with which we are most touched.'[1]

This is helpful as far as it goes, and admirably describes the type of affective prayer that should develop from the use of the colloquies in the first method of prayer laid down by S. Ignatius Loyola and also from the practice of the second method, in which a well-known prayer is used phrase by phrase, dwelling on each phrase as long as the attention can be sustained. There are, however, other ways in which the prayer of the affections will arise, such as through the regular use of the Office, from which certain phrases will stand out and specially move the heart so that they will be carried over into the general prayer of the day; from the observation of nature; and from the spontaneous action of the natural intuition which may suddenly offer a thought which may possess the attention and move the affections.

People who use affective prayer, whether they know what they are using so that they can give it a name, or just happen to pray that way, had very much better not worry about its nature but should persevere in praying, leaving it to the Holy Spirit of God to lead them forward. There is a real danger that the soul should occupy itself in trying to estimate where it is or what it is doing on the ladder of prayer.

The foundation of all education in prayer must be laid in humility and mortification and built up with steady perseverance. There are no short cuts in the spiritual life except those which God Himself provides. We have to work out our salvation 'with fear and trembling.' There are no hard and fast divisions in the spiritual life except one that does not concern us in this book, namely the clear-cut distinction between all ordinary prayer and infused contemplation. In ordinary prayer the soul is responding to the prevenient grace of God— that is, grace going before and leading the soul to make its own acts through its free will. The soul is inspired, instructed, and supported by the Holy Spirit, but its operations and knowledge are carried out and gained through the ordinary channels of its natural faculties. It must therefore use the powers which God has given it of perception, memory, under-

[1] *The Spiritual Teaching of Father Louis Lallemant, S.J.*, p. 256. (Burns, Oates & Washbourne, 1928.)

standing, emotional feeling, and imagination, so as to bring into activity its will to depend upon God, and through such exercise to increase its capacity to know and love the Love which first loved it and gave it the power to respond in freedom of will.

Affective prayer grows out of formal meditation perfectly naturally and simply. Meditation, after all, is only an exercise in method, through which the reflective powers are used upon some subject or aspect of life in order to secure an accurate knowledge about it and to discern the will of God for the individual in relation to it. It is a technique of thinking and there are many different methods. They will all lack their purpose if they do not move the feeling of the individual to talk to our Lord and his saints about the subject, and train the individual to wait upon God to know his will. This is clearly brought out in the method of meditation which S. Ignatius Loyola makes use of in his exercises. The exercise does not stop with the discursive reasoning wherein the powers of the soul—memory, understanding, and will—are employed, or even with the discovery of some resolution which should be made. The meditation is intended to lead on to what S. Ignatius calls the colloquy, that is, the talking over what has been understood with our Lord and the saints, and to the formulation of a prayer for assistance in carrying out the resolution. With practice the colloquy will naturally take a predominant part in the exercise and it will be carried out through the offering and ejaculation of simple phrases, which the emotional life will continue to express after the thinking is done. These ejaculations may be carried into the day and should be returned to often. It was S. Francis de Sales who instructed the meditator to choose from the morning exercise some bouquet with which he could refresh himself during the activities of the day. These bouquets, or ejaculations, are affective prayer, for they are a work of the affections. It has been suggested that S. Bernard of Clairvaux was accustomed to write out some simple and penetrating phrase from Scripture and hang it on a board in his cell so that he could continually return to it in order to keep his attention fixed and penetrate deeper and deeper into its meaning. Whether or not S. Bernard himself did this, as Mr. Eales suggests in a footnote in his translation of the Sermons on the Song of Songs, the method is an excellent one and one would like to think it had such high authority. This choice of some particular text or phrase to brood on is an aid to affective prayer, but needs the support of reading and study, if no formal meditation is being practised at the same time, which serves to provide the material in the mind to fill out and enlarge, through the aid of the Holy Spirit, the particular thought which is held before the attention through repetition.

HOW TO USE AFFECTIVE PRAYER

Souls differ in temperament. There are some whose main attraction is to the many activities through which they live their life in relationship to the world and persons around them. There are others who find themselves more occupied with the inner meaning of those relationships, their ultimate purpose, and their own inner life as part of the whole pattern. The former are by nature actives, the latter more contemplative. The author of *The Cloud of Unknowing*, in discussing the differences between the two, suggests that in the prayer life each has two stages or ways, and that these overlap so that the first way of the active is not known by the contemplative, nor is the second way of the contemplative known by the active, so long as he remains an active; but the second way of the active and the first way of the contemplative are much the same.[1] This explains why some people from the nature of their temperament may find that the active methods, which are so generally prescribed for beginners in the prayer life, not only do not meet their case but get them nowhere. If they should find they are using kinds of prayer which for the active may be considered somewhat 'advanced,' they are not therefore entitled to consider themselves at all proficient, for they are in fact the veriest beginners in their first way of prayer. 'Advance' in prayer, if this word is allowable, is not to be registered by any aptitude or facility in prayerful expression, but is more safely measured by the less obvious standards of detachment, unselfishness, and a disciplined life.

To make use of an old metaphor: as a bird flies on its way borne up on two wings, so the soul in its flight toward the goal of its being, union with God, needs both the prayer of desire and the discipline of self-denial. It is not the purpose

[1] Cf. *Cloud of Unknowing*, Chap. xxi.

of this book to direct in the ways of discipline but only to
provide material for prayer. Perseverance in prayer, as prayer
comes, is of more importance than seeking a diagnosis of the
particular type of prayer used. However, it is well to realize
that there are times when affective prayer is easy and there
are times when, to say the least, it is hard.

Whenever a simple affection is adequate to hold the attention it is sufficient, and there is no need to go on from it. To do
so would indeed check the flow of affection. When there is no
sense of emotion or stirring of the perception through the
prevenient action of the Holy Spirit to secure the action of the
will, something must be presented to it to move its activity and
preserve its freedom. The will requires a solicitation to bring it
into effective operation. This is secured by controlling the
attention through the deliberate presentation to the perception
of some truth of fact or project of desire, to which the will may
make its assent. Many people find it difficult to find thoughts
or words to use in this way, so that the careful reading over and
use of ready-made phrases may be of great assistance. In this
book there are phrases to stir the thought which by repetition
may serve to draw out the user's own intuitions and give
opportunity for the Holy Spirit to develop them, and also ready-
made words with which to speak to God and the saints. If
the heart is stirred by their use, well and good. If not, they
may be used to keep the attention occupied, and as acts of the
will to combat distractions and so enable one to wait on God
till he gives feeling or knowledge.

In the first case some word, phrase, or object perceived
causes or elicits a response in the heart, and this response is
expressed by an act of affection. In the second case the soul, un-
moved and unaided by any natural feeling, expresses its
devotion by formulating acts, or a series of acts, which are
made in faith in order to express its dependence on, and love
for God, Creator, Redeemer, Sanctifier. The danger here is
trying to force the emotion to secure feeling, and so either strain-
ing the faculties or even producing imaginative phantasies for
the self to feed upon, instead of relying on the Holy Spirit to
support the faith in perseverance. Because of this danger it is
better to use the word 'conscious' rather than 'forced' to describe
this operation of affective prayer, for it is the conscious act
of the self, aided by prevenient grace, putting before the will

a perception of intellectual truths, not felt but formulated by rational faith, so as to elicit acts of free will in the various operations of prayer, whether penitence, worship, thanksgiving, supplication, or intercession.

The value of using set exercises and ready-made phrases is that for many people, even though the heart is moved, it is difficult to find words to express the incoherently-felt movement, and the words both provide understanding and give meaning to the soul's activity. The words increase devotion as they help us to appreciate the truth both of what moves the heart and also what should be the nature of our response. If words fail and successive thoughts cease, we should hold the attention of the heart as long as it is supported by the guiding thought, for as S. Augustine writes: 'God hears the heart, not the voice; we do more by groans than words.' But it is most necessary to remember that as soon as the attention flags or the will fails in holding on to the God-directed intention, then it must be renewed by some new act, or repetition of the same act; otherwise a state of inertia or day-dreaming may overcome the soul. This must be most carefully avoided; as also must overstraining by the multiplication of acts which are inspired by self-full desire, for they will serve to 'hurt the head' and to hinder the dependence and surrender of true devotion. It is advantageous to have before one a series of short vocal phrases, each complete in itself but linked with others in a common theme, so that as soon as the attention fails, or we have exhausted for the time the possibilities of the particular thought, we can go on easily to the next, or at times use whole sections to quicken devotion according to the need and attraction of the moment. We must learn to observe a wise freedom, as a learned and discreet priest, W. B. Trevelyan, wrote in the original Preface to the devotion in Chapter II: 'Such prayers as this book contains not only help us to pray directly for a special subject, but they pray round it as well and set us thinking,' and 'Such prayer may indeed be only the first step on the ladder of prayer but a step it certainly is, and those who set it aside as unworthy of them and crave for something more heroic before they are ready for it, are making a grave mistake which may have serious consequences for their spiritual life.'

This may be illustrated by considering the well-known

prayer which forms the introductory exercise to Chapter VII, in which the soul contemplates, that is, looks steadily upon, the wounds of its Saviour. The imagination, aided by the representation of the Crucifix, or through the exercise of the memory, puts before one as an object of perception the fact of the Saviour's wounds and all that follows from them in the way of redemption and renewed life. The result may be a spontaneous movement of the heart which holds the attention and quickens the desire to love, and so easily and naturally draws out the acts of faith, hope, and charity which will be expressed as the heart finds words to express them. If, on the other hand, there is no quickening or movement of the heart as we gaze on the Crucifix, or hold in imagination the thought or image of the wounds by which we and mankind are saved, the impotence of our desire does not take away from the truth and reality of what those wounds are, and the effect which the Passion of our Lord has, and continues to have, upon our souls and the life of men. Knowing this, we can then make acts in faith which express our rational acknowledgement of spiritual truth, and formulate the answer of our free will to that truth.

The place in the prayer life where so many souls fall back is where the spontaneous acts begin to fail, for then souls feel that they have lost devotion and, instead of persevering with conscious acts, get careless and indifferent and neglect their prayer life, and so run the grave risk of losing what they already may possess.

We must choose some statement of truth, some act of heartfelt desire and occupy the heart and will by the repetition of the act of faith, hope, or charity. It may be, if we go through a certain number of these, either provided in a book or gathered for ourselves, one or more may stir the beginning of an affective response; if so we should stop and let the spontaneous act develop if it will, but we must not try to force it merely because we desire to have feelings. What is essential is that the will should be kept responsive by the steady repetition of the acts, so keeping it attentive to God and dependent on grace lest it should fall away into reverie and so be occupied with itself or lapse into some auto-suggestion or quietism. In this kind of prayer distractions are rampant, and they must be ignored and kept on the fringes of the attention through the

B

repeated stirring of the will centred on the phrase or concept of the selected affective act.

Repetition is the essential of this kind of devotion. Through repetition the form of words, from being the limited expression of an immediately perceived intellectual pattern of thought, becomes a true symbol of an ever-extending emotional and volitional reality which gradually unfolds and becomes a possession of the soul. The vocal expression is the refrain of the attention. The repetition of well-known phrases will serve to bring out the depths of their meaning and the fullness of their emotional significance. There are many people who, with a real desire to pray, never bring any spiritual reality to birth in their souls because they turn themselves from book to book, from teacher to teacher, losing themselves in a multitude of different forms of words, spending time in saying many prayers, but praying little. A restless hen that frequently leaves the nest to find a better site, or spends much of her time rearranging her eggs will never hatch chicks; for only a quiet and persistent brooding will enable the dormant life to develop to the birth. In meditation we seek devotion; in affective prayer we find, and yet have to persevere in knocking, so that if the Master of life should of his will open the door of contemplative knowledge we are waiting on the threshold.

THE PLAN OF THIS BOOK

The exercises in this book taken as a whole proceed on a definite plan. They begin with a general dedication of the soul to the Most Holy Trinity, and conclude in the last section of Chapter IX with an affective contemplation of the same mystery of Triune Love by whom creation was made and in and for whom we have our being.

Chapters II and III divide prayer into its component parts, providing exercises for its operation under different headings, in each case prefaced by a general introduction which should be used either wholly or in part as a general setting of the attention before using any selected section of the chapter.

In order to pray it is not necessary to divide one's time and energy or to analyse what one is doing, but if we are to learn to pray with understanding it is helpful at times to proceed by rule and division in order to ensure that we are not leaving out some necessary part of the fullness of devotion.

The fundamental principles of prayer are comparatively simple. They comprise the recognition and acceptance of the fact that man is a creature who possesses a capacity to respond of his own free will to his Creator, and the carrying into effect of that capacity in the appropriate activities of creaturely life in body, mind, and spirit. This implies that both the attitude and the action must be one of dependence. As the creature's life is not originated by itself but given, it also follows that the out-going of the creature is only a response to the gift of the Creator. Not to pray is unnatural, and only the prayerful man can be said to be fully human. All prayer must also be in penitence. The mere fact that prayer is not spontaneous must force upon man's attention that his whole nature has fallen short of the divine purpose and that he is possessed by sin and sinful inclinations and desires. These two marks of prayer are universal and must be implicit, if not actually expressed, in every other expression of relationship in the soul's communication with God. It is the clear perception and the steady practice of the fundamental two-fold relationship of a creaturely penitence which alone secures the objectivity of prayer and preserves it from becoming a subjective exercise in self-reflection, or the expression of self-centred desire. It is right and fitting to pray for oneself, but this action must not be separated from the actuality of community. Personal sanctification we must desire and pray for, but it is for the glory of God and for the sake of others and not as an isolated possession. That is the error of all the theosophists, who would attain to spiritual knowledge by self-training and not by way of humility and self-loss.

Some users of these exercises may be disappointed that there are not more examples of conversations with, or co-operation in devotion with the saints. This is not from any lack of appreciation of the importance of such prayers, but because it is my settled opinion that individuals are better left to find their own friendships and attachments and should learn to talk with the saints simply and naturally without any special direction. I have therefore left it, except in a few places, for the individuals who use this book to develop spontaneously and naturally their recognition of the presence, aid, and comfort of that host with whom we unite ourselves whenever we lift up our heart in the Holy Mysteries of the Church's Liturgy. The pilgrim's road would be indeed empty if all those who had passed that way, and had attained the heavenly felicity, were forgotten by those who now struggle through things temporal seeking those things that are eternal. It can be no detraction from the worship and praise of Almighty God to realize that there is a great company that praises and worships him, which has passed by the same way that we are traversing in this present time. Earthly worship is not the only worship that ascends to God. Our worship on earth can only be a very poor reflection of that perfect adoration in the heavenly places where saint answers saint in ceaseless praise. If that is so, and if we believe in 'the communion of saints,' we should not fear to recognize the fact and rob our prayers of the truth we assert in the Creed. Therefore to omit from a collection of prayers for pilgrims all reference to that heavenly company who watch over and pray for our labours in the arena wherein they won their victories would be a betrayal of spiritual truth. To omit devotions wherein our Lady and the saints find a fitting place would deny Christian tradition. Naturally and properly a devotion to our Lady will take first place, but after that each individual will find his own special friendships, attachments, and devotion. It is natural to our loneliness and fitting to our humility to ask the prayers and care of our friends. It would be indeed unneighbourly if we restricted this operation to the limited circle of those whom we could know in the flesh, and ignored the number of those whom we might come to know by faith. Like every other kind of knowledge, material or spiritual, knowledge of the saints can only be made real by experiment. If we leave them out of our life and thought they will be unreal to us, but if we cultivate their friendship then, and only then, shall we find that they are indeed near to us, and that the honour we pay to them is the honour due to God's work in accomplishing their holiness.

Chapter IV is intended as an introduction to the use of the Psalter as a storehouse of material for affective acts. Chapter V is a devotion directed to our Lord, for a Christian life without a deep and persevering love for the Person of its Saviour would be a misnomer and not a life of discipleship. The most profound difference between Christian prayer and all other expressions of the soul's desire for and communication with God, is that the Christian speaks directly to a living and present Master, the ascended Lord, who is true man of our manhood as well as Very God. There is therefore an intimacy in the prayer of the Christian disciple which, to those who do not understand, may sometimes seem exaggerated or unnatural, but which is the perfectly natural and logical result of the knowledge of the Saviour's promise, 'Lo, I am with you alway.' The pilgrim, whose life is already hid in the Kingdom which is Christ's, though still working out his salvation with fear and trembling in the temporal order, wherein the kingdom of the prince of this world is in the process of being overthrown, is only capable of progression in so far as his life is being transformed into the fullness of Christ. He walks therefore by faith in and with him who is his Saviour and his life; therefore, if he would progress in his vocation of Christian virtue, he can only do so as he consciously and deliberately surrenders himself, not only to the leading of the Good Shepherd, but to union with the Personal Life of Jesus who has overcome sin and conquered death.

The devotions of this chapter are only suggestions for intimate conversation; they are not intended to be followed too closely, but rather to serve as signposts to lead each individual who may use them to follow out the prayers that God may give to him. They should be used as vocal prayer, though silently, following up the idea expressed in the phrase, *by its silent offering*, and not leaving one phrase until either the mind begins to wander or the resources of devotion contingent on that phrase are for the time exhausted. Do not strain, and do not labour; love and adore, and give God time and silence wherein to speak to you and draw you to himself. 'It is a great art to know how to hold converse with Jesus, and to know how to detain him in the soul is great wisdom. Be lowly and restful, and Jesus will be present with you. Be devout and quiet, and Jesus will remain with you.' So writes the author of the *Imitation*;[1] therefore let us study to be collected, humble, quiet, and restful in our prayer time, and so learn to carry the same temper into our daily life. Dwell quietly on each thought as it is presented to the understanding and make a definite offering of each to our Lord.

We should feel the truth and reality of prayer better if we more often definitely regarded it as an intimate conversation

[1] Book II, Chap. viii. 3.

between the soul and the Redeemer, who sees all, knows all, understands all, who is ever waiting for us, however dimly we may realize his presence. If we are to bring God into all we do and think, and so fulfil our purpose in the world, we must give time, not to inactive brooding, but to loving prayer. If we make time for quiet talks with God, for our acts of love, reparation, and spiritual communion, then we shall be able in the midst of the bustle of affairs to remember that he is with us. This knowledge may be obscure, and only by faith. Walter Hilton reminds us that:

'He is in thy soul, and never shall be lost out of it. Nevertheless, thou art never the nearer to Him till thou hast found Him. He is in thee, though He be lost from thee; but thou art not in Him till thou hast found Him.'[1]

Whether we have knowledge or not, the Lord seeks each soul he loves, to satisfy her, to fill her, if she empty herself for him, with himself. The Bridegroom of the soul waits to adorn the beggar bride so that she is lovable and attractive to himself. She must empty herself. Such is the teaching and experience of the saints. To give up self can never be easy; love is the only sure guide to show the way. Love grows by loving, driving out all else, and love alone can answer Love.

Friendship with our Lord, the acknowledgement of discipleship, must lead to following in his footsteps, so Chapter VI singles out six words describing the saintly character. To achieve such a character, growing in grace by grace, the words must not only be words to us, but possessions lived for, and lived with, until our whole life is marked and conditioned by their acquisition. The exercises have been arranged in sections under the heading of these words with a general introduction to be used before each, based on the submission of the understanding, affections, and will. Intellect alone is sterile; affection, unregulated by intellect, is purposeless and only impotent desire; while will, without intellect and affection, is without point or object. From the surrender of the disciple and the desire for holiness the new step is to that knowledge of which S. Paul speaks, whereby we may know our Lord and the power of his resurrection, and the fellowship of his sufferings, becoming conformed unto his death.

Chapters VII and VIII are meditations with affective acts

[1] *Scale of Perfection*, Book I, Chap. xlix.

to lead the soul to approach, and to unite itself with our Lord in his redemptive activity of self-sacrificing Love, whereby we may willingly offer ourselves to fill up what is left over according to his will and appointment. Our life in Christ is an achievement as well as a gift. It is by the renewing of our minds in co-operation with grace that we walk or progress towards him and come to be in him. Surely it is here that we may find the reason for what is so obvious in life, that many who are regular in prayer and sacrament seem to grow so little in holiness and unselfishness; that many who long to put some sin or evil habit finally behind them still walk beneath its shadow, and may even come to doubt the power of Christ to set them free. What is it that holds these poor souls back? They desire holiness, long for holiness, but there it ends; they do not put their wills to it, they do not work for it by mortification and taking every opportunity of practising the virtues they need. Their failure is in love, for love is always of the will more than of the affections; love must do and suffer, else it is not love.

The last chapter may not be so generally useful. It should not be attempted except by those who find that the repetition of single words, weighted with emotional content, helps to keep down distractions and hold the will steady in its response in faith to the love of God. If repetition of this simple type is not to degenerate into a psychological use of *mantras*, the words used must be filled with emotional and intellectual meaning. I have therefore filled out the chosen words in many ways so that by using them, resting on the various affective expressions, the users may so charge the words that it may become for them sufficient to repeat the word; and that so doing it may both dilate the heart and hold fast the will.

THE IMPORTANCE OF SELF-DISCIPLINE

In general the user of the exercises should note that the prayers are arranged in short sections, many of which can be detached from their surroundings and may be used as complete devotions in themselves. This is intentional, for it is often more advantageous to return again and again to the same form, if and as long as it will serve to express devotion, not through the stimulation of feeling but in heartwhole surrender. We should never forget the counsel of Père Grou:

'We must not measure the reality of love by feelings, but by results. Feelings are very delusive. They often depend on mere natural temperament, and the Devil wrests them to our hurt. A glowing imagination is apt to seek itself rather than God. But if you are earnest in striving to serve and endure for God's sake, if you persevere amid temptation, dryness, weariness, and desolation, you may rest assured that your love is real. As men advance in the interior life, they learn to indulge less and less in self-dissection, even as regards their love of God—they are content to give themselves up to Him in this matter as in all else—to love Him without any conscious dwelling upon their love; and this is the higher and purer form of love.'[1]

It is not enough to be indifferent to things of the body, which often leads only to harshness and lack of consideration for others. It is far more important to be indifferent to the feelings of the soul. To complain almost petulantly when spiritual consolation is withdrawn, as some do, or to grumble and give up trying to pray when dryness and distraction seem to be the only reward, is the surest way to hinder the grace of God in its work of unifying and perfecting the human life. Likewise to take refuge in physical discomfort for its own sake, or restless activity for others just for the sake of doing, is a subtle and deadly form of self-assertiveness. The best mortification for many is to be quiet and patient, to study to let life flow evenly and without any violent emotional strain. As a stream unruffled by the rocks below more perfectly reflects the sky, so the undisturbed heart may turn to God with little conscious effort except that the will is continually moved by the habitual formulation of acts or expressions of love and dependence. If the mortification of things exterior is needful for the liberation of the spiritual, even more necessary is the mortification of the spiritual so that only desire for God, and a will surrendered to him in all things should remain. Many fail by refusing to persevere in prayer and in their way of life when they seem to themselves to be unable to pray. They turn back to a dependence on worldly things and seek an outlet for their energies in a round of distractive occupations, interests, and exercise of affections dissipated upon the creatures, to their own unhappiness and the impoverishment of the life of God's kingdom.

[1] H. L. Sidney Lear, *The Hidden Life of the Soul*, p. 127 (Rivingtons, 1889).

Let the soul, then, that has been called away from the more discursive and exciting prayer of the mind to the simpler and shorter expression of the heart in the ways of affective devotion, have no fear when there is no feeling or taste in its devotional work. When prayer has become a labour, it is often most real, for it is then that the will by its perseverance and adherence to God in faith is able most perfectly to prove its devotion and express the disinterestedness of true love.

If some of the devotions in this collection give a superficial impression that they are world-forgetting and only recognize the 'I and Thou' of the soul and its Saviour, it must be understood that a true love of God involves of necessity a love for all his creation. To leave God's world and the needs of one's fellow men on one side is no true prayer life. This age of human history is dying from man's ignorance of God and his will, and no lover of God can turn his eyes from the pity of man's tragedy, or do else but pray incessantly, 'O God, if man did but know thee, then all things would be put straight.' It is only when the material has been brought into subjection to the spiritual that men who are enslaved to the material can be freely served and impartially helped. To be free to serve man in God's way, the Christian must first detach himself from the human ways of local loyalties and strong natural emotions, and learn the justice, truth, and impartiality described in the scripture: 'He sendeth his rain on the just and the unjust.' Such a discipline is unpalatable to the natural man, and likely to be misunderstood, for he thinks of it as the death of nature, when in reality it is the death of all that separates; it is the birth of liberty and the fulfilment of the natural in the power of the spiritual. Without this rebirth and redirection prayer will be cold and formal, or self-expressive and self-interested. A humanism that ignores the necessity for the individual struggle for holiness and loses sight of the unique claims of God upon personal devotion will have little power to overcome the inertia and temptations of the material environment, and so will have little energy to serve others, except in ways that imply little or no real or sustained self-sacrifice. If God is to be known, the world and self have to be put into their proper place: that is, put in subjection to God. To die to the world, to lose the life of the individual self-centredness so as to be alive in union with eternal being may seem to be a hard and circumscribing counsel, yet it is the only way to the liberty that possesses the world. To lift the heart in prayer in order to seek a kingdom not made by hands does not mean that the pilgrims, whose hearts are lonely, because their treasure is hid beyond all earthly desire, have turned their backs on the things of the world and all its human complexities. They approach it from another side, that of the eternal, for they must see and feel the tragedy and futility of human life and activity without God as its end and direction, and to know the weakness and sinfulness of their own unaided natural existence, and the need of their dependence upon the supernatural life of union with the Divine Love.

The world has many lovers and God, alas, has few. This is a book for pilgrims who have set their affections on heavenly treasure and are determined to persevere in the way thereto. If it should serve to help any of these to express and to increase their love of God it will have served its purpose. That it may do so is the prayer of its compiler.

CHAPTER I

A DEDICATION TO THE BLESSED TRINITY

O GOD, THOU HAST MADE ME
       THOU HAST REDEEMED ME
       THOU HELPEST ME.
       TEACH ME
       TO KNOW THEE
       TO LOVE THEE
       TO WORK WITH THEE
          THIS DAY AND EVERY DAY.

I

O God, thou hast made me
       and all that is made is of thee:
    there is none before thee
       nor after thee:
    thy Being has neither end nor beginning
       nor any succession of time:
       thou art immeasurable, incomprehensible,
          alone in thy Godhead.

And I—
       thy creature, brought into being in the order of
          created life
       made for thy praise and glory
       to serve thee in loving freedom
       to possess all things in thee and for thee,
          my God, my all.

O God, thou art in all and through all,
       yet not a part of that which is created by thee:
    thou art existence
       by and through which all that is possesses form
          and has beginning:
    thy works are eloquent of thee
       yet are not thee,

therefore they reveal thee
and worship thee:
thou art before them, beyond them,
they exist because thou art
nor can they rival thee,
my God, my all.

O God, thou art my God
thou madest me
thou art eternal, uncreated,
the living fire of Love
in whose creative power all being has its source:
thou art the Light
wherein the visible 'becoming' doth proclaim
thy invisibility:
thou art the energy
through which each separate part of thy
creation acts
whether in the ordered pattern of nature's law
or through the individual liberty of
freedom's gift:
thou art the Way,
the only way wherein thy creatures can be
rightly free:
thou art the Truth
whereby intelligence may measure life,
emotion feel the fullness of relationship,
that life may answer Life
and will may freely find its end
in love's dependence,
my God, my all.

And I—
my power to respond to thee
is not my own.
Thou gavest it.
I love, because thou lovedst first,
and to thy love
my love, the love thou gavest,
must answer Love,
my God, my all.

O God, teach me to know
        that love alone can answer Love,
        that all that is not love
        must dwell apart from Love,
        a living death within the darkness that is not thy
           love,
        for love alone can dwell within the Heart of Love
        and love is all the life of Love.
        Love is the Way, the Truth, the Life.

And I—
        a sinner in the world of sin,
        so full of love for self,
        twisted, torn, tormented by multitudinous desires,
        the slave of every wandering impulse from without.
        Within—a place of conflict
        restless, unsatisfied,
        a stuttering will, which would but cannot act
           with certainty:
        the things I would I do not,
        the things I would not, those indeed I do,
        a sinner in the world of sin.
        But yet within the warring conflict of disunity
        I know thou lovest me,
        for thou didst give thyself for me,
        taking our human life
        in which thou wast made sin to break the bonds of sin
        through death, destroying death and overcoming him
        who had the power of death.

II

O God, thou hast redeemed me:
        teach me to love thee,
        that all my life may be for thee,
        upheld in thee,
                my Lord, my God.

O God, thou hast redeemed me:
        draw me to love thee,
        give me the strength, thy strength in me
            to bear the pains of penitence,

to take my cross and follow thee,
to watch and pray
and to endure unto whatever end thou hast
appointed for me,
my Lord, my God.

O Word made flesh
the first and last, the fullness of all time,
without whom was not anything made that
was made,
the Living One, who was and is and shall be,
who was dead and is alive for evermore:
true man, whose body bears the prints of love's
self-sacrifice,
the marks of nail and thorn, of spear and scourge:
true God, effulgent brightness of uncreated light
binding eternity and time in one new man—
my Lord, my God.

Teach me to love thee, not for thy gifts but for
thyself:
inform my memory
that all my thoughts may tend to be of thee:
illumine my understanding
that I may know thy inmost dealings with
my soul:
stir up my will
that it may ever move to meet thy call,
dependent
humble
penitent
for thou alone redeemest me from death.

Saviour, who gave thyself for man,
endured the cross, despised the shame
for joy of Love's completest unity:
draw me to love
that I may feel, within thy oneness,
the separate unity of all who are in thee:
that I with them in charity may worship thee
the Lamb
whose Blood outpoured for ever pleads for those

who know thee not or will not answer love
in Love's completest unity:
whose prayer proclaims the end and purpose of
        becoming,
that it might reach unto the oneness of
    created unity
in thee made one with uncreated
    Love in unity of Trinity,
in praise and worship everlasting,
where angels and all saints for ever cry:
    Holy, Holy, Holy, Lord God of hosts,
heaven and earth are full of thy glory,
        glory be to thee, O Lord most high.

O Life, who lifted up man's death
        that death might be no more
        and Satan's rule be overcome,
    we supplicate thee for the souls of men that
            live in death.
    By cross and passion we appeal,
    O God make speed,
    O Lord make haste,
        that all mankind may come to know thee
        and knowing, love thee
        that sin may cease.

Lord of the field which is my soul,
        teach me to know how I may answer love
            in laboured husbandry,
        nor leave concealed the rocks of self-
            possessiveness within
        that will betray thy word in temptation's day
            of heat;
        nor leave uncut, undug, the growth of thorn and weed
            that Satan sows and this world cultivates:
        teach me to dig my field,
            to dig both deep and wide
            nor weary from the task thou settest me,
            that I may know myself
            and thou create in me
            the harvest of thy life.

O Lord, my only end,
>> restless is the heart that knows not what it needs
>>> to find its life's completeness.
>> In passionate desire it loves, yet knows not love:
>> its love is restless torment for release from love's
>>> complaint—
>> a passion for completeness that seeks release
>>> yet does not know the give and take of charity,
>>> and cannot know the truth of love
>>> till passion that is born of self is dead.
>> Take thou my mind
>>> that it may be renewed, transformed unto thy mind,
>>>> so that I may have understanding of thy Way:
>> take thou my feelings and imagination
>>> that they may be restored to health,
>>>> redirected to thy Truth;
>> take thou my will
>>> that it may act consistently for thee,
>>>> obedient, humble, and secure
>>>>> at rest in thee.

Jesus, whose birth as human child the angels sang
Jesus, whose passion lawgiver and prophet in the mount
>> foretold
Jesus, whom men refused
Jesus, who called his own and gave them power to endure
Jesus, who sent the Holy Spirit to live within his Church
Jesus, before whose feet the doubting apostle bowed
Jesus, at whose presence the seer in Patmos lay as dead
Jesus, my Lord, my God
Jesus, my strength, my life, my food, my end,
>> without thee I am nothing—
>> thou art my all.
Jesus, I am not free, but bound to thee:
>> for me thou didst pay the price of sin
>> for me thou gavest thyself to draw my love to thee:
>> thou gavest all to win my all, such as it is,
>>> my sinfulness and separation from thee.
Jesus, if I rebel, punish me,
>> if I flinch from suffering, encourage me,
>> if I endure, reward me with thyself.

Jesus, thy grace alone can satisfy
        the love thou givest me,
        that I may give my all to thee
        in charity.

III

O God, thou helpest me,
        dwell thou within my heart:
        it is not mine to use just as I would,
        it is remade a temple for thy use
           through Calvary.

O God, thou helpest me,
        help me to be myself—
        the self thou wouldest have me be:
        convict my sin
        enlarge my righteousness
        bring to thy judgement every act and thought of mine,
        that with a conscience sensitive
        I may maintain thy fellowship
           through penitence and aspirations after truth.

Paraclete,
        true personality within the triune Mystery of God
          proceeding from the Father and the Son,
          in glory equal
          with the Father and the Son
          in co-eternal majesty,
        be thou my guide,
        attune my ear that I may hear thee speak
          thy word unto the Church and to my soul.

Most Holy Spirit, Comforter,
        the ever present guest within the soul
        the voice of conscience
        the call to holiness
        the strength that holds the will,
          if it convert
          and turn from self to godliness:
        thou art most close, most intimate,
          bring me to quietude

C

that I may hear within my soul
what thou dost say.

It is my restless self-absorption,
my undisciplined approach to outward things,
my fears, my hopes,
that dull the hearing of my soul
that make me dread the silence
    wherein thy voice is heard.

Most Holy Spirit
        I have no life unless thou light my way
            to show the riches that are tawdry loss
            and all the multitude of things
            that have no value in the sight of God
            and hinder and confound the pilgrim's way.

Most Holy Spirit,
        enlighten thou the mirror of my soul
        that I may hold it steady in thy ray
        to see the piercing beauty of thy truth
        in righteousness and judgement manifest,
            and come to holiness as thou dost guide.

Most Holy Spirit
        burn thou my soul
        that I may turn myself within
        and find thee there,
            a still light,
        lest rich in mine own conceit
        and many plans
        and wayward idlenesses
        I should dread the darkness
        wherein I cannot act or plan or be self-full—
            that very darkness which is the light
        wherewith thou dost envelop me
        and draw me to consent,
        if I should only pause
            and give myself to thee.

Paraclete, most Holy Spirit
        most close to every one thou dwellest:
    thou art the inward movement of every good
    thou art our striving after righteousness
    thou art our aspiration after holiness
    thou art the love that turns our soul from death to
        life, converting us:
    thou art the voicing of the Father's call
    thou art the inextinguishable ground of faith
        in every soul
    thou art the drawing of the eternal Son
      by which we are brought home unto the Father
    thou art the coinherence that binds creation
        made perfect in the fullness of Incarnate Love
    thou art the deep compassion that maintains and
            orders life
        within the world's confusion made by wills that seek
            their own in disobedience:
    thou art the glory that illuminates the saints
        made perfect in the Word of God,
            through suffering purged
    thou art the judgement that brings all evil to
            conclusion
    thou art the quickening of the angel hosts
    thou art the overthrowing of all prideful separation
    thou art the catastrophic liberty of love
        in love's dependence;
    thou art the fire that purges souls through love
        from dross of lesser loves and stain of sin
    thou art the inspiration that conforms the will
        to see and follow ways of expiation
    thou art the Light of heaven
        wherein we see the Father and the Son
    thou art the energy that lifts the soul in purgatorial
            prayer
    thou art the fire that burns in hell
        in judgement on the self-full isolation
        that would dwell apart
        in pride-full supremacy of self.

Thou art—
    O Spirit, holy, blessed, dear, and wonderful

thou art—
  all words must fail to say
  just what thou art!
  The soul that turns within
  in humble restfulness dependent on thy will
  may know
  and knowing praise and love thee,
    the Comforter.

Comforter
  sent by the Saviour to indwell his Church
  to form his Body, soul by soul,
  and guide its way
  unto the consummation of the end.

Comforter
  who takes the things of Jesus
    to show them unto me.
  Teach me to live thy way
    the way of Jesus
    step by step
    grace following grace.
  Teach me to be a stranger to the aims of world-
    possession.
  Teach me to be a traveller through the vanities
    that pass,
    that all my way be Jesus' way
    and thou the Guide,
      my Comforter.

Most Holy Spirit, Comforter Divine
  through thee the life of prayer is made complete
  through thee the suffering pilgrimage is made
    joyful
  through thee the darkness is made light:
  illumine thou my life, inspire my prayer,
  be thou the unity that makes me one,
  that I may be all prayer,
  one coinherence with my Source and End
  one coinherence with the world of men and
    nature's order

one wholeness in myself
    purged, restored, reunited in the life
    from which man fell
    and which the Passion of our Lord restored
    a temple for thy Majesty.

MOST HOLY TRINITY
    TO THEE I BIND MYSELF
    TO THEE, IN THEE, BY THEE
    I MAKE MY PRAYER:
    DRAW ME IN THE QUICKENING MOVEMENT OF THY LOVE
    UNTO INCREASING KNOWLEDGE
    OF THE MYSTERY OF LOVE WITHIN THYSELF
    THAT I MAY GROW IN LOVE
    DEPENDENT, FAITHFUL, HUMBLE,
    FOR MY LOVE TO THEE
    IS THAT THOU GIVEST ME.

Chapter II

A PILGRIM'S MEED OF PRAYER AND PRAISE

I

COMMENDATION AND DEPENDENCE

Remember, Christian Soul,
        that thou hast this day and every day of thy life
                        God to glorify
                        Jesus to imitate
                        A soul to save
                        A body to mortify
                        Sins to repent of
                        Virtues to acquire
                        Hell to avoid
                        Heaven to gain
                        Eternity to prepare for
                        Time to profit by
                        Neighbours to edify
                        The world to despise
                        Devils to combat
                        Passions to subdue
                        Judgement to undergo.

Take, O Lord, and receive my whole liberty,
        my memory,
        my understanding,
        all my will,
        all I have and possess.
Thou hast given it to me;
        to thee, Lord, I restore it;
        all is thine;
        dispose of it entirely according to thy will.
Give me thy love and grace,
        for this is enough for me.

I commend into thy hand, O Lord
    my soul and my body
    my mind and my thoughts
    my prayer and my vows
    my intentions and my attempts
    my going out and my coming in
    my words and my works
    my senses and my limbs
    my life and my death.

        Christ be with me
        Christ within me
        Christ above me
        Christ below me
        Christ before me
        Christ behind me
        Christ on my right
        Christ on my left
        Christ all about me
        To guard and direct me
        That each meeting
        Each work undertaken
        May be by, with, and in Him
           done to his glory.

O Lord, Jesus Christ, my God,
    what shall I say unto thee?
O Lord, I will speak unto thee,
        I who am but dust and ashes:
        I have sinned against thee
        I have been ungrateful
        I have been unfaithful.
           Have mercy.

Would that I had never hindered the work
        of thy grace in me,
Would that I had always pleased thee,
Would that I had always obeyed thine inspiration
        and thy will.
        Wash me
        Cleanse me
        Heal me
        Make me holy.

> Come, O Holy Spirit, fill the heart of thy child,
> and enkindle in me the fire of thy love and
> understanding, that I may know, love, and
> accomplish what is thy will for me.

II

CONTRITION

Jesus, my Saviour,
>> my sins hide thee from me
>> the shame of my face hath covered me
>> my confusion is daily before me.

Jesus, my Lover,
>> I have grieved thee
>> I have pained thee
>> I have wounded thee
>> I am worthy of hell, even the lowest place in hell.
>> I have sinned most grievously by deed, word, thought.
>> Thou forgivest me, yet I sin again and again.
>> My life is sin, I am all sin unless thou live in me.

>> Help me, most kind Saviour, and give me grace that
>> I may worthily lament my misdoings, for between
>> us there stands a bitter evil, my worldly habits
>> and my own desires.

Jesus, what can I say to thee?
>> Thou madest me—and I have made myself an outcast.
>> Thou gavest me life—and I have used it for my own
>> ends.
>> Thou gavest me understanding—and I have ignored
>> thee
>> and thought on the passing joys of the world and
>> studied fleshly delights.
>> At thy chastening, since I might not escape from it,
>> I have groaned against thee.
>> If I have kept from open sin, it was not for love of thee,
>> but dread of man,
>> for my health and comfort,
>> for my own convenience.
>> How can I answer?

How can I give account to thee
  of my time,
  of my deeds,
  of my talents,
  in that day when thou shalt call for an account?
I have presumed on thy mercy.
I have nothing to answer.

Jesus, thou callest me to repent:
  I have been self-satisfied.
  Thou commandest me to seek perfection:
  I have been content with myself.
  Thou enduredst pain and suffering for me:
  I have been easy with myself;
  Thou wast mocked, despised, and insulted for me:
  I have enjoyed praise and sought human approbation.
  Thou humblest thyself for me:
  I am all pride and self-seeking.
  Thou drawest me, uplifted on the Cross:
  I am so slow in coming.

O merciful Saviour, have pity, where shall I go,
    to whom shall I go, save unto thee?
  Have mercy; thy mercy is so full and large that all
    who ask receive, nor could they ask, but thou
    in mercy givest them the thought they ask.
  Save me, loving Lord, from my just reward,
    the misery that I have earned,
    the eternal sorrow of hell I deserve.
  Save lest I should burn for ever,
    seeing with open eyes
    the wounds that I have given thee.

Lord, I repent.
  Help thou my impenitence,
  pierce, rend, crush my heart.
Lord, as thou art loving, give me tears.
  Who shall lighten my darkness if thou pity me not?

  How fearful is thy judgement, O Lord!
  When the thrones are set,
    the angels stand around

and men are brought in,
the books opened,
the works inquired into,
the thoughts examined.

Lord, I repent.
Help thou my impenitence.
Be merciful to me a sinner, the chief of sinners.
Thou Christ, my Saviour Christ, Saviour of sinners,
of whom I am chief.
Despise me not, despise me not, O Lord,
who am called by thy Name.
Look upon me with those eyes
with which thou didst look upon
Magdalene at the feast
Peter in the hall
the thief on the cross;
that with the thief I may entreat thee humbly:
Remember me, Lord, in thy Kingdom;
that with Peter
I may bitterly weep;
that with Magdalene
I may hear thee say 'Thy sins which are many
are forgiven.'

III

ADORATION AND PRAISE

O God, one God in Trinity, and Trinity in Unity,
I worship thee.
Father, Son, and Holy Spirit: in glory co-equal, in majesty
co-eternal:
I glorify thy mystery.
O God invisible, Creator and Sustainer of all that is:
The Word is life, light, and life of all men.
The Spirit guideth all things
to reflect thy glory.
O God, infinite, perfect,
I praise thee in the Unity of Trinity.

O incomprehensible Trinity:
>grant that I, which am but dust and ashes,
>may render in a soul properly humbled
>due worship unto thee.

O most merciful Trinity,
>three Persons, one God, Father, Redeemer, Sanctifier,
>teach ⎫
>direct ⎬ me, who hope in thee.
>help ⎭

O adorable Trinity, would that I could love and praise thee
as perfectly as the angels and saints love and praise thee!
Since I cannot praise thee as I ought, do thou
>deign most perfectly to praise thyself in me.

Thou, O Lord, art Life, filling all things with light.
Thou, O Lord, art Love,
>dwelling in thy angels
>and in thy saints,
>so as to fill them with all blessing.
Thou, O Lord, art the Chief Good.
>The Eternal Good.
>From whom all good things come.
>Without whom nothing is good.
Three Persons, One God,
>ever to be adored and worshipped,
>>Creator
>>Redeemer
>>Comforter.

IV

ADORATION AND THANKSGIVING

I adore thee ⎫
I praise thee ⎪
I glorify thee ⎬ O precious Jesus
I bless and thank thee ⎭

>for all thy mercies and benefits to me
>and all mankind.

I bless and thank thee most especially that for me
      thou didst condescend to become Man:
      thou wast born in a stable
      thou didst endure poverty and want
      thou didst suffer agony with bloody sweat
      thou wast mocked, scourged, unjustly condemned
      thou wast crowned with thorns,
        stripped before men
        and nailed to the Cross,
      thou didst hang upon the Cross
        all wounded and racked with pain,
      that bearing my sin
        thou didst suffer desolation
        and death, and wast laid in the grave.

O sweet, precious Jesus, my salvation, grant me that I may
  love thee with most fervent love.

I worship thee, beholding
      thy love toward mankind,
        for thou didst bear all our sins upon the Tree:
      thy humility,
        for thou didst empty thyself, taking the form of a
          servant:
      thy obedience,
        for thou wast made obedient unto death:
      thy pity,
        for thou wentest about doing good and healing all:
      thy penitence,
        for thou didst fast forty days and nights:
      thy humanity,
        for thou didst weep at the tomb of Lazarus
        and didst console the widow of Nain:
      thy poverty,
        for thou hadst not where to lay thy head:
      thy devotion,
        for thou didst spend whole nights in prayer:
      thy fatherly care,
        for thou didst multiply the loaves and fishes
        and didst feed the hungry in desert places:

thy loveableness,
    for thou art such that all men desired to see thee:
thy gentleness,
    for thou didst absolve the adulteress, kiss the traitor
    Judas, and pray for thine enemies:
thy rectitude of heart,
    for thou didst not seek thine own glory but that of
    the Father:
thy patience,
    for thou didst say 'Father, thy will be done,'
    and as a lamb before the shearers wast thou dumb:
thy generosity,
    for thou givest us thyself: 'Take, eat, this is my
        Body, drink ye all of my Blood.'

O sweet, precious Jesus, my salvation, grant me that I may
        ever hold myself close to thee, the Way,
        ever think on thee, the Truth,
        ever live in thee, the Life.

O Jesus, I adore thee
    I love thee
    I give myself to thee,
        O most loving Saviour.

V

INTERCESSION

Most merciful Jesus,
        have mercy on thy Church:
        convert the sinners
        reform those living evil lives
        recall the heretics and schismatics
        help all in necessity and trouble:
        show thyself in mercy on the heathen
            and those who know thee not:
        till all things are reconciled unto thyself.

I commend unto thee
        my wife, husband, children,
        my parents,

my brothers and sisters and their children,
my relatives,
my friends,
my servants, my employers,
my benefactors,
my well-wishers,
all those who have a claim on me,
the management and labourers in any business
from which I draw wealth,
my neighbours,
all whom I have met with and those whom I am to
meet.
Be with all those who have asked my prayers.

I pray unto thee for
the sick,
the suffering,
the desolate,
the lonely,
the despairing,
the hungry,
the ill-clothed and needy,
the poor,
prisoners and captives,
those with none to pray for them,
those whom I have ever offended by word or deed.

Make all men pleasing unto thee,
stablish the Faith,
convert the nations,
give peace in the world.

Grant to the living pardon and grace,
to the faithful departed rest and light.

'I am naught; I have naught; naught I seek nor covet
but the love of Jesus.'

Sweet, precious Jesus, my Lord and my God,
kill in me whatever is displeasing to thee.
Thou art my Maker, my Redeemer, my Lover.

Thou art the Master of my inmost soul.
Thou madest it for thyself; deal with it
   and all of me as thou seest fit.

Give me true humility
        true obedience
        true meekness
        true patience
        true love.

Grant me a clean heart to see thee,
  detachment of spirit to serve thee,
  true recollection to know thee.
Conform my spirit to thy blessed human nature.
Conform my soul to thy holy soul.
Conform my body to thy most pure body.
Free me from all that prevents my union with thee.
Grant me the living spring of waters in my soul
    so that I may know thee clearly,
        love thee ardently,
        cleave to thee in closest union,
        rest in thee,
not for any merit of my own, for I am
altogether wretched and cast-away, but
for the praise of thy name.

Hear me, O my God, not according to my will,
    but according to thy good pleasure.
Hear me in the way best fitting to thy honour
    and my salvation.

        Guard thou my soul
        stablish my body
        elevate my senses
        direct my converse
        form my habits
        bless my actions
        fulfil my prayers
        inspire holy thoughts
        pardon the past
        correct the present
        prevent the future.

Give me thy peace which passeth all understanding,
and knit me so close to thee that I may never be parted from
thee—

Jesus, my Lord, my Love, my Life.

VI

A RECOLLECTION OF THE ANGELS AND SAINTS

O all ye saints of God,
O all ye blessed angels,
I greet you and ask of you your prayers.

Mary, Mother of God,
take pity on me an outcast,
pray for me, that I may be bound to thy Son
with perfect love,
pray for me, that I may become wholly
according to his heart.

Good angel, given to me as a guardian,
who beholdest the Father's face,
bear with me, guide me,
fulfil in me the Father's will.

O all ye holy ones, whose joy is ever to behold the face of God,
pray for me
that I may ever please the King most high.

VII

SELF-SURRENDER

O Saviour,
I am nothing,
I desire to be below all
to be the servant of all.

Teach me sincere charity, so that I may love all,
and particularly those people
who are distasteful to me, and those
who have injured or wronged me.

Be thou within me to strengthen me
   without me to guard me
   over me to shelter me
   beneath me to stablish me
   before me to guide me
   after me to forward me
   round about me to secure me.

Fill me with thyself,
   for I love thee alone,
I choose thee above all.
I give myself into thy hands, ready to bear
   any disgrace, any injury,
   any contempt or reproach,
   any trial or pain,
strengthened by thy grace
and for the glory of thy Name.

Lord Jesus, may I know myself and know thee,
   nor desire anything else except thee,
   may I hate me and love thee,
   may I do all for sake of thee,
   may I humble me, exalt thee,
   may I ponder nothing except thee,
   may I die to myself that I may live in thee,
   may I receive whatever happens as from thee,
   may I banish self and follow thee,
   and ever desire to follow thee,
   may I fly from me, may I fly to thee
   that I may deserve to be defended by thee,
   may I fear for myself and fear thee
   that I may be among those chosen by thee,
   may I distrust myself and trust thee,
   may I be willing to obey on account of thee,
   may I cling to nothing but thee,
   may I be poor for the sake of thee.
   Look upon me that I may love thee,
   call me that I may see thee
   and in eternity may enjoy thee.

D

VIII

LOVE

O God,
>my God and my All,
>the perfect satisfaction of my desires,
>what can I want save only thee?
>Thou art my only and unchangeable good.
>Thee only ought I to seek.
>Thee only do I desire.
>Draw me after thee.
>Burn me in the fire of thy consuming Love.
>Pity my wretchedness,
>>my desolation,
>>my ignorance,
>>my blindness.
>
>Forgive my laxity,
>forgive my failures to amend,
>restore me and make me thine.

Good, merciful Jesus,
>thou hast set me in the midst of the world
>thou seest that I am beset with dangers
>thou orderest me
>>to be pure in the midst of corruption
>>to be humble in the midst of praises
>>to be poor in the midst of riches
>>to be holy in the midst of sins:
>>in the midst of enemies to be unconquered,
>>that living in the world I am not to be of the world,
>>that resting on earth I am to be of heaven.
>
>Without thee I fail, without thee I am lost,
>>without thee I cannot obey thee.
>
>Strengthen me to do thy will,
>>supply me with thy grace,
>>direct me,
>>make perfect that wherein I fail.
>
>Make me thine, and only thine, so that
>>thou mayest be able to find delight in me.

O most precious Jesus, my Lord and my God,
　　　　take me to be thy servant,
　　　　teach me so to love thee
　　　　　　that all my labours be to love thee,
　　　　　　my hope, my longing, my reward.

　　　　Be thou within me
　　　　　　　above me
　　　　　　　below me
　　　　　　　before me
　　　　　　　behind me
　　　　　　　on my right
　　　　　　　on my left
　　　　　　　all round about me.

　　　　Fill me with thy life, plunge me into the
　　　　　　abyss of thyself.
　　　　I love thee alone
　　　　I choose thee above all.
　　　　Fill me with thyself.

Make me thine and only thine, O most precious Jesus,
　　　　my Lord and my God.

IX

A TALKING OF LOVE

The Beloved speaks
　　I am the light of the world; he that followeth me shall not
walk in darkness but have the light of life.

The soul replies
　　　　My Jesus, I pray thee,
　　　　　　give thou thy light to my heart,
　　　　　　that burning with light unquenchable
　　　　　　it may enlighten my darkness
　　　　　　and lessen the darkness of the world.
　　　　My Jesus, I pray thee
　　　　　　that thou wouldst give to me such light
　　　　　　　that I may always behold thee,
　　　　　　desire thee,
　　　　　　look upon thee,
　　　　　　and love and long after thee—
　　　　　　　　my Jesus.

The Beloved speaks

I came to cast fire upon the earth ; would it were kindled already.

The soul replies

O Jesu, O Sacred Heart,
    burning with Divine Love
send into my heart
    a spark of that fire
    which burneth in thee;
excite in me a burning and a flaming spirit;
impress upon me
    the seal of thy Love
    that I may worthily perform thy work.

The Beloved speaks

If any man will come after me, let him deny himself and take up his cross daily and follow me.

The soul replies

Heart of Jesus, be my peace
Thy wounded side my home
Thy broken feet my following
Thy pierced hands my guiding
Thy crown of thorns my exceeding rich reward
Thy cross my daily toil
Thou knowest all, O my God
Thou knowest my wretchedness
Thou knowest that I love thee.

Chapter III

CREATURE AND CREATOR

PREPARATION

'*The custom of speaking to God Almighty as freely as with a slave, caring nothing whether the words are suitable or not, but simply saying the first thing that comes to mind from being learnt by rote by frequent repetition, cannot be called prayer: God grant that no Christian may address him in such manner.*'

S. *Teresa of Avila: 'Interior Castle,'* Chap. I, 9.

O God, my God,
  thou seest me,
  thou didst make me,
  for thee I exist
   and have my being
   as thy creature.

O God, my God,
  what is man that thou regardest him?
  He is dust and to dust he must return.
  Yesterday he was not,
   to-day he is,
   to-morrow he is gathered in to death,
   a passing moment in the flux of time.
  Yesterday unknown, unborn, not yet begun:
   to-morrow dead, though still his deeds and thoughts
    live on in their effect on other men.
  To-day he lives with liberty of choice
   to seek and formulate the ends and purposes of life:
  To-morrow he must face thy judgement.

O God, what is man that thou regardest him?
  A living soul
   created free, that he might worship, thank,
    and correspond with thee.
  A living soul
   whose liberty of choice transcends the bounds
    of time and space,

whose liberty of choice to answer thee
  endows thy creature,
  which yesterday was not
  and to-morrow must endure the pains of death,
with apprehension of thy timeless and eternal
  Being.
A living soul
  whose freedom is to make response to thee,
    his sole eternal end,
    in praise
    and reverence
    and service,
    so to save his soul
    and use creation for thy glory.

Man's life is not his own
  but God's good gift
  that it might be the conscious mirror
  of God's own loveliness and liberty,
  in freedom formed to make a free return
  to use creation for creation's end
  the glory of the uncreated Deity.

Man's life, through man's own liberty of choice
    and answer,
  lies under judgement
  bound and crippled through the choice of sin:
  made free to answer 'Yes' to a true freedom,
  yet in that freedom free to answer 'No'
  whereby, through disobedience, sin doth reign
    in place of man's true liberty to God:
  whereby the love of God becomes to the sinful soul
    the wrath of God against the sin.

Lord, hear my prayer
    a sinner's prayer:
  a broken and a contrite heart thou wilt not despise.
    Teach me true penitence.

Lord, hear my prayer
    because thyself, within the body of our servitude,
    hast suffered all our sin
    and called me to turn again and live.
      Teach me to answer Love by love's obedience.

Lord, hear my prayer
because in thee I make my prayer:
my life and liberty restored in thy own gift.
Teach me to live according to thy will.

My life is doubly not my own
to squander as I will:
my life, created and redeemed by thee
once forfeited and once restored
is thine, not mine,
because thou didst pay the price.
I am the bondslave of my Lord.

CONVICTION OF SIN

'*A good man finds sufficient cause for sorrow and for tears . . . the more strictly he examines himself the greater ground for sorrow he discovers.*'

Imitation, Book I, Chap. xxi.

Father, forgive, for I have sinned against thee,
not once, but many times.
Thou didst give to man the precious gift of loving thee
and I rejected thee, loving myself.
Thou knowest that we are but dust:
pity, pardon, spare.

O God, my God,
Thou didst create a human heart for a meeting place,
didst make it thy very own, true flesh,
didst break it once for all for man on Calvary.

My Lord and my God,
thou didst remake a meeting place for love,
when human love had lost its way and turned
from love,
in thy own heart and being
true man, true God
wounded for our sins of separation
through death destroying death.

Thou hast restored the liberty of man once lost
by thine own perfect choice as man
obedient to the Father's will.

Thou showest us thy wounds,
my Lord and my God.

Jesus, I behold thee wounded for our transgressions,
my sin thy pain, my guilt thy agony.
Before the eyes of thy mercy, at the feet of thy tender love
I lay open all my heart and my spirit, and offer them to thee
that thou mayest do with them as seemeth best in thy sight.

I am not worthy, yet thou didst suffer for me
I am not worthy, yet thou callest me
I am not worthy, yet thou hast stooped to come
beneath my roof.
Thy Body and thy Blood thou givest me, thy life my life,
that I may hold thee close in love's embrace, my guest,
my saviour, and my friend,
Hide me in the depth of thy heart, reign in the midst of mine.
Not my will but thine be done, O most loving Saviour,
in me, by me, in all that concerns me,
in time and in eternity.
Take me to thyself, ever to love thee
on earth and in heaven with thee for ever.

Breathe, O breath of God, and make me thine, speak thou
within my heart, that my prayer be thy prayer,
my words thy words, my will thy will.

O God, I trust in thee, Father, Redeemer, Sanctifier.
May I ever be very little, lest by regarding myself
I fall away from thee.

WORSHIP, ADORATION, AND PRAISE

'*God alone—the eternal and incomprehensible, who fills all things—
is the solace of the soul and the true joy of the heart.*'
Imitation, Book II, Chap. v.

My God, my all,
Maker of all the stars of heaven, of the immensities of space,
of the aeons of time; my Maker, Father, Lover, thou
knowest that I am dust, thou knowest that I love thee.

O God, thou art my God,
  I am blinded by the darkness of myself, lost in deserts of
    man's own making.
  I adore thee, unseen, I reach out to thy love.
  Despise not the work of thy hands, make me obedient,
    patient, and fit for such work as thou willest me to do,
              my Father, my King.

Deity supreme, all powerful, most wise and most righteous,
            most compassionate to all who repent,
            in love most severe to all who offend;
  Aid my repentance, deepen my sorrow, grant me the gift of
    true tears, and ever to know my condition as a stranger
    and pilgrim on earth, a wayfarer far from home; so that
    ever sighing for thee, I may hasten the quicker, strive
    the more earnestly, labour the harder, to advance daily
    in the way of salvation.

O God, who holdest me in life, my sustainer,
  grant me to serve thee alone, before all that is of use or
    beauty upon earth:
  grant me to rest in thee alone, using all that I find only
    for thy sake, my God and my all.

Word eternal, by whom the worlds were made, before whose
            glory the angels adoring bend and shield their sight:
Majesty too awful for human comprehension, save only
    beneath the veil thou didst assume as our Saviour and our
    brother.
Jesus, in thy true humanity thy deity I praise, and in thy
    sacramental Presence the Godhead I adore.
Jesus, I adore thee, stooping to the human birth, true manchild
    born of Mary both mother and maid.
Jesus, I adore thee, child in the manger cradle, cherished by
    the Virgin's care and by Joseph, guardian of thy infancy.
Jesus, I praise thee in the perfection of thy childhood.
Jesus, I adore thee, by simple shepherds and the wondering
    cattle worshipped, receiving homage from the Eastern
    kings.
Jesus, I praise thee for every human breath thou didst breathe,
    true man, yet very God.
Jesus, I adore thee, alone in the wilderness with the wild beasts,
    ministered to by angels.

Jesus, I praise thee that thou hast borne our sorrows, in all
ways tempted as we are.

Jesus, I adore thee, homeless and a wanderer, walking steadfast
to Calvary.

Jesus, I praise thee for every word of teaching, for every
power of healing.

Jesus, I adore thee, in the garden bowed beneath all sin,
accepting all the Father's will.

Jesus, I praise thee for thy victory over sin and death, for thy
restoration of humanity to God.

Jesus, I adore thee, reigning from the Tree, passing through
Hades, harrowing hell.

Jesus, I praise thee for my soul restored, washed in thy precious
blood, gathered into thy wounded side, made one with
thee.

Jesus, I adore thee, risen, triumphant, ascended Saviour, true
man, true God, Lamb slain from the foundation of the
world.

Jesus, I adore thee, for ever dwelling in thy Church.

Jesus, I adore thee, thy new creation's life and food.

Saviour, burning fountain of everlasting love,
    reigning in heaven, glorious on thy altar throne.

Jesus, lover and friend, to thee be all my love, my life, my all,
for it is all thine own.

Paraclete, we worship thee.
    Without thee silent were our praise; thy moving voice is
    the whisper of our hearts, the burden of our prayer.

    Breathe thou, O Holy Spirit, on all souls, that every child
    of life may sing thy praise, who art with Father and with
    Son, one God, eternal, strong and free, immortal holiness.

Love reigns
    we serve, God rules:
    we die, Christ lives:
    nothing are we, the Spirit sanctifieth:
    wherefore to God the Father
                through the Son
                in the Holy Spirit's power
    be all praise, all service, all love
    from us and all creation for ever and for ever.

THANKSGIVING, BLESSING, AND GRATITUDE

'They asked the lover if his Beloved had need of aught. Yea, he answered, of those who will love and praise him, and extol his surpassing worth.'

Ramon Lull, '*The Lover and the Beloved.*'

Father, I thank thee
    that I am thy child.
Redeemer, I thank thee
    that thou didst give thyself for me
    and dost live in me.
Life-giving Spirit, I thank thee
    for thy indwelling in the temple of my soul.

O God, who loved thy world so dearly that the only-begotten
    Son was given to save us all
    I thank thee for Jesus, made true man and born a child of
    Mary.
    I thank thee for Jesus, tempted in all ways as we are, yet
    without sin.
    I thank thee for Jesus, moved with compassion, weeping
    human tears.
    I thank thee for Jesus, shrinking from death, surrendered to
    his foes.
    I thank thee for Jesus, nailed to the Cross, rising from the
    dead.
O Love, who givest all, help me to give all to thee.

Saviour, teach me in all things to give thanks, accepting every-
    thing that comes as from thy hand, flying from self-love,
    self-pity, clinging close to thee; abiding thus unshaken,
    constant in my gratitude for life and love and comfort of
    thy grace.
    Woe is me, my life I have accepted as my own, my talents
    mine to use or hide,
    forgetful whence I came or whither I go.
    I have robbed God of life, of time, of opportunity,
    wherefore my place on Calvary's hill is with the thief.

Saviour, speak thou the word of mercy and forgive my lack of
    gratitude.

So late I come to render thanks
　for life, for all created things,
　　the heavens declaring thy glory, the earth thy
　　handiwork,
　for my fellow men, for all who love me,
　for baptism and the manifold gifts of grace,
　for my washing from the stains of sin,
　for my place within thy holy Church,
　for the heavenly food, my hope of immortality.

Saviour, nothing would I have except thou grant it me; give me
　the love to thank thee with, for without thee nothing can
　I render thee, no offering can I make except thine own;
　accept thyself, it is my purest gift.

O God, my God, Monarch Divine, Almighty Power, Wisdom
　above all knowledge, limitless in all thy works, fathomless
　abyss of Being, Beauty of all beauty, Strength of all
　strength, Truth of all truth, the riches of all who seek
　thee, Beginning and End of all who serve thee; to thee
　we, who receive from thee, render again what thou
　givest.
　Be thou ever magnified within our hearts.

Blessed and praised for ever be our God, from whom comes all
　the good that we speak, or think, or do.
　　　　Blessed be God.

SUPPLICATION AND INTERCESSION

'*In thee . . . I place my whole trust and refuge; on thee I cast all my
tribulation and distress, for I find everything is weak and unstable
which I behold out of thee.*'

　　　　　　　　　　　　　　　Imitation, Book III, Chap. lix. 3.

Father, who gavest thy Son for me
Jesus, who givest life to me
Spirit, who sustainest me
　　accept my will, and make it thine.

Thy will be done, on earth as in heaven.
Triumphant certainty I have that thy will is done
 if I but ask according to thy will.

So ask I nothing of myself
 but by thy Passion I appeal
 that thou shouldst guide my prayer
 to pray with thee.

Conqueror of unconquered might,
 to thee I lift my trembling hands
 to thee I bring myself to be made new
 to thee I bear all those who ask of me my prayers
 to thee I offer all the bitter strifes of men to heal
 to thee I bring the endeavours of thy Church to fructify.

 Not I but thou bear up my hands, pierce thou them with the
 nails of love to share thy Cross, that lost in thee my prayer
 may find fruition in thy life.

 Mystery unsearchable, that thou, the Victor over sin and
 death, dost wait for us to share thy sacrifice; that through
 our prayers thou shouldst reach out to other men.

 On Calvary's hill I then implore
 by thy wounds five, thy will be done:
 by hand, by foot, by riven side,
 by broken heart, by thorn-crowned brow,
   thy will be done.

Love, Incarnate, Love Divine,
 inflame the hearts of all who love thee, that alive to thee
 and dead to self they may make manifest thy loveliness
 throughout the world, and through their sufferings united
 to thee may draw souls to thee, to satisfy thy thirst for souls
 and spread the kingdom of thy love.

Love Incarnate, Love Divine,
 calm thou the seas of this world's tumult, and bring thy
 Church to the fair haven of thy peace.

Save, pitying Saviour, for there is nothing in thought or will or deed in whatsoever we sinful creatures think or do, speak or write, that may turn to the profit of man's soul, for of us without thee cometh nothing but filth and sinfulness.

As to Peter in the waste of waters, stretch forth thy hand and hold us up, calm thou the storm without, within be thou our peace.

Eternal Love, the ground of all beseeching, raise up, we pray thee, strong intercessors who shall never depart from before thy face, but shall give thee no rest, and shall take no rest till thou establish and till thou make thy kingdom come in all the earth.

Chapter IV

AN EXERCISE FROM THE PSALMS

I

MY GOD

'*My God and my all. To him who understands, this saying is enough; and to say it over and over again is delightful to him who loves.*'

Imitation, Book III, Chap. xxxiv. 1.

My God.

O God, my God.

O God, thou art my God.

My Father, my God, my strong salvation.

O Lord, my strength, my redeemer.

My God, my rock, my defence, my Saviour, my shield, my refuge.

O Lord, my defender.

O God of my righteousness.

My Shepherd.

Hear, O thou Shepherd of Israel.

He shall be our guide unto death.

II

CREATOR AND GOVERNOR

'*From me small and great, poor and rich, as from a living fountain, draw living water, and those who render me a free and willing service shall receive grace for grace.*'

Imitation, Book III, Chap. ix. 2.

O God, how glorious are all thy works, in wisdom hast thou made them all.

The earth is full of thy riches.

The heavens declare thy glory, the firmament showeth thy handiwork.

Thou art from everlasting.

A thousand years in thy sight are but as yesterday, seeing
    that is past as a watch in the night.
Thou, Lord, hast made me glad through thy works.
Thou holdest our soul in life.
All my fresh springs shall be in thee.
Thou searchest the heart and reins.
Thou art about my path and about my bed.
Thou spiest out all my ways.
There is not a word in my tongue but thou knowest it.
Thou knowest all my desire, my groaning is not hid from thee.
Show me thy ways, O Lord, and teach me thy paths.
How glorious are thy words, thy thoughts are very deep.
O Lord our Governor, how excellent is thy Name in all the
    world.

III

RIGHTEOUS AND MERCIFUL

*'Place your whole trust in the Lord, may he alone be your fear and
your love. He himself will answer for you, and will do well, as it
should be for the best.'*

Imitation, Book II, Chap. i. 3.

Thou art gracious and righteous, yea, thou art merciful.
Thou art righteous in all thy ways, and holy in all thy works.
Help me, O Lord my God, O save me according to thy mercy.
Thou art the same and thy years shall not fail.
Therefore under the shadow of thy wings will I rejoice.
I am horribly afraid for the ungodly that forsake thy law.
My eyes gush out with water because men keep not thy law.
For the comfortless trouble's sake of the needy and the deep
    sighing of the poor.
Put my tears in thy bottle, are not these things noted in thy
    book?
My help ever cometh of thee, O Lord, who hast made heaven
    and earth.
For thou comest to judge the earth, with righteousness to judge
    the world and the people with thy truth.
My trust is in thy mercy.
How excellent is thy mercy, O God; with thee is the well of life;
    in thy light shall we see light.

IV

JUDGE AND SAVIOUR

'*There thou wilt show me to myself, what I am, what I was, and whence I came; for I am nothing, and I knew it not. If I am left to myself, lo I am nothing, and all weakness. But if thou suddenly dost look upon me at once I am made strong, and am filled with fresh joy.*'

Imitation, Book III, Chap. viii. 1.

God is judge himself.
Thy judgements are in all the world.
Behold, Lord, how that I am thy servant.
Deal thou with me, for thy mercy is sweet.
Thou art nigh unto them that are of a contrite heart.
For thy Name's sake be merciful unto my sin, for it is great.
Be merciful unto me, heal my soul, for I have sinned against
    thee.
Cleanse thou me from my secret faults.
Set a watch, O Lord, before my mouth, keep thou the door of
    my lips.
I am utterly purposed that my mouth shall not offend.
Show the light of thy countenance and we shall be whole.
In thee is my health and my glory, in thee, O Lord, is my trust.
My heart is joyful in thy salvation.

V

HELPER AND REDEEMER

'*That which surpasses all is, that thou thyself hast deigned to serve man, and hast promised to give thyself to him.*'

Imitation, Book III, Chap. x. 3.

O God, thou art my God, early will I seek thee.
Out of the deep have I called unto thee, O Lord; Lord, hear
    my voice.
Preserve me, O God, for in thee have I put my trust.
Make my darkness to be light.
Yea, the darkness is no darkness with thee.
Hold thou me up, and I shall be safe.
Have mercy upon me, for I am weak; heal me, for my bones
    are vexed.

E

Bring my soul out of prison that I may give thanks unto thy Name.

Despise not the work of thine own hands.

Behold how that I am thy servant.

Thou hast broken my bonds in sunder.

I will trust in thee,

For thou art the God of my refuge.

O visit me with thy salvation.

Thou art a place to hide me in.

Because he hath set his love upon me, therefore will I deliver him:

I will set him up, because he hath known my Name.

O God, be not far from me; O God, make haste to help me.

God is my hope and strength, a very present help in trouble.

I will not fear though the earth be moved.

Salvation belongeth unto thee, O Lord.

Yea in thee, O God, have I put my trust; I will not be afraid what man can do unto me.

Thou art my helper and redeemer, make no long tarrying, O my God.

Thou shalt show me the path of life, in thy presence is the fullness of joy.

Thou makest peace in my borders.

Thou fillest me with the flour of wheat.

I shall not die, but live, and declare the works of the Lord.

VI

MY ALL

'*Unite me to thyself with an inseparable bond of love; since thou alone dost satisfy the one who loves thee, and apart from thee all things are empty.*'

Imitation, Book III, Chap. xxiii. 10.

Thy face, Lord, will I seek.

O God, wonderful art thou in thy holy places.

My soul thirsteth for thee, my flesh also longeth after thee.

Whom have I in heaven but thee? there is none upon earth that I desire in comparison with thee.

Like as the hart desireth the water brooks, so longeth my soul
for thee, O God.

My soul is athirst for thee, O God, yea, even for the living God.

Comfort the soul of thy servant, for unto thee do I lift up my
soul.

My heart and my flesh rejoice in the living God.

Yea, the sparrow hath found her an house, and the swallow
a nest for herself where she may lay her young: even thy
altars, O Lord of hosts, my king and my God.

One day in thy courts is better than a thousand. I had rather
be a door-keeper in the house of my God than dwell in
the tents of ungodliness.

My soul trusteth in thee, and under the shadow of thy wings
shall be my refuge.

Thou art the strength of my heart, and my portion for ever,
O God, my God.

*Almighty Father, Eternal Love, grant to us such knowledge of our
poverty and dependence that we, coming to realize our true nothingness,
may live only in thy love, and so praying always may offer thee not
our unworthiness but thy love in us; through Jesus Christ our Lord,
who with thee and the Holy Ghost art one God, world without end.*

CHAPTER V

A PILGRIM'S PRAYER TO JESUS

'It is a great art to know how to hold converse with Jesus, and to know how to detain him in the soul is great wisdom. Be lowly and restful, and Jesus will be present with you. Be devout and quiet and Jesus will remain with you.'

Imitation, Book II, Chap. viii. 3.

O Jesus,
    blessed Jesus,
    thy Name is above every name
        more excellent,
        more sweet,
        more lovely.
    At thy Name all things that are created bow.
    How wonderful are thy works;
        thou madest them for thyself.
        Thou madest me,
        thou gavest me freedom,
          that I might love thee or desert thee,
          cleave to thee or deny thee.
    Ever thou lovest me,
        but I forget thee, and forsake thee, I scorn and despise thee,
        passing thee by, wounding thy love.

O Jesus,
    blessed Jesus,
    I gaze on thy Cross,
O Saviour suffering to draw my love:
        was ever love like thine, or thanks so poor as mine?
        Thy hands are outstretched for love of me and all mankind, and with my sin I have pierced thee and keep on wounding thee;
        Bitterly I sorrow, deepen my penitence.
        Give me tears that I may weep.
        Give me strength that I may amend.

Take me to thyself,
>> keep me in thy wounds,
>> ever mindful of thy presence,
>> ever to love thee,
>> in pain and in bliss,
>> on earth and in heaven,
>> with thee for ever.

O Jesus,
>> blessed Jesus,
>>> hear me,
>>> nor ever let me be separated from thee.
>> Thy mercy is so plenteous;
>>> pardon my guilt.
>> Thy love is so compelling;
>>> draw me to thy feet.
>> Thy stripes which are for my healing
>>> bid me come closer.
>> Thy Flesh broken for me,
>> thy Blood freely offered,
>>> are my pledge and my hope.
>> Saviour most patient, strong, and kind,
>> mercy of God so near to me,
>> mercy that would wrap me round
>>> and shield me,
>>> and take me,
>>> and bind me
>>> in newness of life,
>>>> draw me, unite me to thyself
>>>> that I may come to fullest love,
>>>> and live and love with thee.
>> Saviour, have pity, smite me and wake me;
>>> my soul is dark with the darkness of sin,
>>> my hands are bound with chains of their making,
>>> my back is bowed with the burden of guilt,
>>> my eyes are blinded with the night of myself.
>> Saviour, pity, stir me and take me,
>> break thou my bondage,
>>> my self-pleasing,
>>> all that comes between us,
>>> all that makes me fear and dread thee,

all that blinds my sight and hides thee from me;
    for I love thee,
    and would give thee
    all thou askest,
    and would ever only do thy will.

O my Saviour,
clasp me close and closer to thee.

O Jesus,
        blessed Jesus,
        I adore thee, I worship thee;
        teach me to love thee, O Love of God.
        Love stooping to thy human birth,
                satisfied with the stable,
                going about doing good,
                Healer of the sick,
                Forgiver of sinners,
                triumphant in pain,
                reigning from the Cross,
                Conqueror of death,
                ever pleading in heaven,
                perfect beyond all perfection.
        Love incarnate, Love divine,
                embracing all,
                pitying all,
                seeing all,
        look thou upon me,
                cleanse me,
                burn me,
                give me to love thee,
                kindle me with the flame of thy everlasting love,
                        O Love of God.

O Jesus,
        blessed Jesus,
        thy presence benign is awful and sweet;
        where thou art not is chaos and void,
            an ocean of discord where no one may find rest.
        Only in the ark of thyself is fullness of peace.
        Depth beyond depth of living stillness,
        height beyond height of burning love;

Truth, Life, Way,
my Lord, my God,
    inflame me,
    burn me with thy love so that I may love thee,
    dispel my confusion,
    cleanse me from my secret faults,
    from all that holds me back from thee,
    from all that hinders my service for thee,
    from all that I am or do that keeps others
        from coming to thee.

O Jesus,

blessed Jesus,
my soul thirsteth for thee,
my flesh longeth for thee,
yea ever for thee, the living God.
My trust is in thy mercy,
thou art my confidence,
    the strength of my heart,
    my hope for ever.
With thee there is a well of life,
    and in thy light shall I see light,
    with thee is no darkness or shadow of turning.
Grant that, ever meditating upon thy perfection,
I may more and more be conformed to thee,
    so that I may love thee better,
    so that I may serve thee better,
    so that cleaving to thee I may win others for thee.
Grant that, ever feeding upon thee,
I may be surely grafted in thee,
    so that my life shall be ever thy life,
    and my fruit thy fruit.
I am nothing,
    thou art all.

O Jesus,

blessed Jesus,
my soul is fickle and wayward,
    it would ever cling to thee, and never leave thee,
    but ever it wanders from thee, filling itself with
        empty delights,
    as a gossamer it is driven on the winds.

Thou only abidest, steadfast, unchangeable,
in thyself thou makest all things new;
thou madest me; in thee I had new birth, and
thou hast made me a new creature.
Touch me, hold me, for I am thy own,
lest I drift hence and be no more seen,
burning for ever in the agony of losing thee.

O Jesus,
blessed Jesus,
I would never leave thee;
inflame my heart so that it shall ever know thee.
Jesus, thou hast done everything for me;
I have nothing to offer thee;
purge thou my heart,
burn thou my soul,
cleanse me,
all of me,
so that I may be empty for thee.
Thou askest of me a gift in return for thy love,
thou askest me to surrender myself to thee,
wholly and without condition;
willingly would I give it thee,
it was never my own,
for thou gavest it me,
and I love thee,
and above all I desire thee.
But I have spoilt it and marred it;
it is less than nothing,
I have made it worthless, abominable;
but take me,
and keep me,
for thee only I love,
thee only I desire.

Jesus, my Love, my God,
breathe into me the desire of loving thee
only,
before all things,
before myself;
let it be my joy that thou reignest eternal
that thou art all perfection,

that all things are thine,
that I am thine.
Thou alone art the satisfaction and reparation of
all sin.
Thou alone makest the satisfaction for wrongs
done unto thee.
Thy heart is broken, pierced for sin and for
the healing of sin.
Join my heart to thy heart,
so that with thee and in thee
I may be enabled
to bear and to offer
thy love to thee,
for my own sins and neglects,
for the blindness and hardness of men's hearts that
pass by thee,
for thy betrayal at the hands of those who call
thee Lord,
yet seek their own will, crucifying thee afresh,
and putting thee to an open shame.
In thy heart hide me
that I may share thy grief,
and loving learn to love thee.
Give me but one desire,
one task,
one end,
just to love thee,
Jesus, my Jesus.

O Jesus,
blessed Jesus,
I adore thee, I worship thee;
teach me to love thee, O Love of God.
Jesus, my Saviour most pitiful, most merciful,
thou veilest thyself,
lest my nothingness should perish before thy face.
Take me,
do with me as thou willest;
I am not my own;
thou boughtest me with a price,
thou feedest me with thy life,

thou holdest me in life;
what can I say unto thee?
what can I give unto thee,
thou that art my joy,
    my hope, my all?

O Jesus,

blessed Jesus,
thy presence is not hidden from those who love thee;
    we know thee present,
    we love thee present,
    we adore thee present.
Thou didst deign to take our flesh,
    and dwell among us,
    so that man might behold thy glory in the world.
    Thou givest thyself, Body and Blood,
        to be our food,
        and to be ever with us,
        so that we might find thee,
        and adore thee,
        present with us,
        tabernacled in our midst.

O Jesus,

blessed Jesus,
give me love to answer love,
    love that is beyond all speech,
    so that my love, which is indeed thy gift, enkindled
        by thy flame, within my soul may answer Love.
Give me but one desire,
    grant me but one purpose,
    just to love thee.

Jesu I love,
Jesu I adore,

hide me in thyself,
wrap me in the stillness of thy peace,
    that no voice may be heard,
    no thought conceived,
    but only of thee.

Jesus, my Jesus,

blessed Jesus,
    no words can express the love I would give.

I am nothing, I have nothing;
   thou art all.
Fill me with thyself;
   as the fish is in the sea, so may I be engulfed
   in thee,
      that in thee
      I may move
      and rest
      and toil
      and never leave thee.
O hide me in thyself;
   hold thou me up,
   so that I may only go
   wheresoever thou directest me.

Jesus, my Jesus,
      I would be thy servant;
         trembling I reach to take the cross I must bear,
         for so thou commandest, that each should take up
         his cross and follow thee.
      Hold thou me up
         so that in thy love I may bear whatever of suffering,
         or toil, or hardship, thou mayest appoint.
      I am nothing,
         my flesh faileth,
         my heart fainteth,
         nothing I can bear without thee.

O Jesus, my Jesus,
      thy love is so great,
         so wonderful,
         so precious.
      I would bear all that thou appointest,
         whatever of trial,
         whatever of pain,
         whatever of weariness,
         if such be thy pleasure,
         and if each bring me nearer thee.
      Gladly I give thee whatever I can.
      Thou didst endure the Cross despising the shame;
         thy hands are outstretched with the marks

of thy Passion,
thy side is rent with the tokens of love.

O Jesu,

draw souls,
draw each one I pray for,
draw by the might of thy bitter Passion,
thou victor of death,
reigning to everlasting,
Lamb that was slain,
reigning on Calvary,
reigning in heaven,
reigning in love,
showing ever thy wounds that bring us to bliss,
thy broken Body, thy living Blood :
by the depth of thy Passion draw us to love thee,
that with all nature,
with the saints and the angels,
with Mary most blessed,
with the pure in heart and upright of the earth,
with all thy true children in all ages and places,
we may say:

Thou only art holy,
thou only art the Lord,
thou only, O Christ, with the Holy Ghost, art most high
in the glory of the Father. Amen.

Jesus,

blessed Jesus,
grant me thyself,
that through thyself received
I in thy heart may reign
and thou in my heart reign,
so always, everywhere, O Guest Divine,
even in my worthless heart,
thy name of Jesus may be blessed.
Give me the grace
to cleanse the temple of my being,
to keep it fit and fair for thee,
desiring nothing but to find thee everywhere,
within the soul's depth and secret place,
in all the busy world without.

Jesus, blessed Jesus,
>> draw me to love thee,
>> within thy shadow bring me
>> just to love thee,
Jesus, my Jesus.

Jesus, my Jesus,
>> my Lord,
>> my God,
Jesus, my Jesus,
>> my all,
>> my love.
Jesus, my Jesus,
>> my heart yearneth after thee,
>> my soul thirsteth for thee,
>> my joy,
>> my life,
>> my beginning,
>> my end.

Jesus, my Jesus,
>> no voice I would hear,
>> no thought I would conceive,
>> but only of thee.
Jesu, I adore thee,
>> I worship thee,
>> I love thee.
>> Hide me in thyself,
>> keep me in the stillness of thy peace,
>> give me but one desire,
>>> one task,
>>> one end,
>>> just to love thee,
>>>>> Jesus, my Jesus.

Lord Jesus,
>> The world despised thee:
>> I would honour thee.
>> The world derided thee:
>> I would praise thee.
>> The world blasphemed thee:
>> I would worship thee.

Man betrayed thee:
  I would be faithful to thee.
Men struck thee and scourged thee:
  I would willingly bear suffering for thee.

Lord Jesus,
        light and life of every man, give me thy light that
            walk not in darkness but have the light of life.

Lord Jesus,
        show me this dark world as seen by thee,
            that I may bear thy light to do thy will
            in overcoming darkness.

Lord Jesus,
        I pray thee
            enlighten my understanding,
            inflame my affections,
            that my whole will may be set on thee
            to do thy will,
                    Jesus, my Jesus.

Chapter VI

THE PATTERN OF THE MASTER

PREPARATION

*'For thy life is our way, and by the path of holy patience we walk
toward thee, who art our crown.'*

Imitation, Book III, Chap. xviii. 3.

O God, thou didst make me.
O God, thou hast redeemed me.
O God, thou helpest me.

O God, my God and my all,
   without thee I am nothing, less than nothing,
   a rebel to thy love,
   a despiser of thy grace.
O God, have pity upon me a sinner;
   grant me a new vision of thy love
     and of thy will for me:
   give me stillness in my soul that I may know thee and love
    thee, and grant me strength to do thy will,
O God, my all.

O God, thou hast given bread for my body, and silence for my
   soul.
   How can my body live without bread; how can my soul
   live without silence?

O ocean of Love, stillness profound, light and life of all who
   come to thee, draw me into thy still peace, that all the noise
   of things be stilled and the music of my soul be all one
   harmony, thyself alone, my God, my all.

O God, I am thine;
   move thou my prayer, that I may seek thee:
O God, I am thine;
   stir thou my heart, that I may find thee:

O God, I am thine;
  enslave my will, that I may hold to thee:
  enlighten my will, that I may grow in thee:
  enfold me in thyself, that all my being be to thee alone,
          my God, my all.

O God, thou art my God;
  move thou each separate power of my being, that all its
  occupation be of thee.
Cleanse thou my memory, that it may keep only the impress
  of thy love.
Make quick my intellect, that every active thought may turn to
  thee.
Support my will, that all I do may be for thee,
  joyfully accepting all things in thee, for thee, through thee,
          O God, my all.

Father, I, the prodigal, do turn to thee; seek thou me out
  upon the road, that all my thought and mind be filled with
  thee, and I may find, and finding, love.
Incarnate Love, that died for me, inflame my weak affections;
  that burning in thy purest flame of love, all that is not
  thine may be consumed and purged away, that I may truly
  love.
Thou Comforter and Guide, move thou my will, that, one in
  love with thee, I may in love increase.
O Blessed Trinity, that art the source of all my being, grant me
  such love that, dying to myself, I may return thy love, and so
  thou mayest be my only end, my God, my all.

O God, my Love,
  from thee I come,
  thine I am,
  to thee I go.

O God, thou Mystery of ever-loving love, from Love, to Love,
  in Love,
          O ever-loving God of Love.

O God, thou hast made us for thyself, that we might be the
  mirror of thy loveliness:

thou hast taken our life to be thine own, that we may see
thy beauty as thou wouldst have it be in human form.

O Jesus, God and Man, so draw us to thyself, that lost in thee
we may find life.

Jesus,
Crown of virtue, perfect pattern of the human good, in thy
humility we see the Way thou willest every human soul
to go.
Give us the grace to follow thee, that learning of thy meek
and lowly heart we may find rest, the rest of love,
stillness of an everlasting energy,
self-lost in giving love and love's return.

Jesus,
Light of the eternal Brightness,
Fire of the everlasting Love,
thy awful purity declares the Truth;
help us to die, that by detachment freed from all except
the Father's will we may for ever burn one flame with
thee.

Jesus,
Fountain of life,
Friend, Comrade, King,
who holdest out to us the chalice of thyself,
teach us to feel the beating of thy sacred Heart,
that we alive in thee may know that
our life is dying and our rest is suffering,
our riches poverty, our poverty abundant wealth.

My King, my Love, my only Hope, my Jesus, thy life is all too
clear for those who read, too hard, too high:
grant me thy courage that I may share thy pain.
O Love, who dost awaken souls to journey forth in faith,
leading thy people through the wilderness,
guiding the feet of them that seek through fire and water
so that they may come unto the wealthy place of thy
surpassing love:
grant me thy awaking touch and guidance all the way.

F

Jesus, who dost call thy servants out of the world,
  that they may live within thy heart, the very members of
  thy Body, triumphant through thy Crucifixion;
  too high, too hard the Way, unless, Lord Jesus, thou art
  mine.

HUMILITY

'*Through this virtue more than anything else, all saints were and are
men according to God's heart. In short, in this virtue the whole
discipline of Christian wisdom consisteth.*'

Blosius, 'Sanctuary of the Faithful Soul.'

Learn of me, my Saviour says; learn to rate thyself the servant
  of all living, to hold within thy heart no thought but that the
  Father may be glorified, and so find rest, life and healing for
  thy soul.
Woe is me, I am undone; before thy Way, thy Truth, thy Life,
  my self-complacency, my pride, my indolence, is ever more
  and more revealed.
Touch thou my lips with thy burning fire, burn thou my dross,
  grant me contrition that all my days be lived in penitential
  lowliness.

The cattle's manger cradled thee a helpless babe, no courtiers
  to hail thy reign, but humble shepherds and the old wise
  men.
No tribute, but the gifts offered to declare in symbol the
  truth of kingship, the life of Deity, the way of sacrifice.

My God, so in every heart thou reignest in the depth, hid from
  the pomp of earth, the pride of life, the lustful eye,
  to be accepted or ignored.

The house of prayer, that should have welcomed thee, thy
  rebellious children made a den of thieves, a place of beasts
  and marketing and strife.
And I—how often have I turned thee from the door by pride,
  intolerance, or fear, by greed and avarice.
And I—when I should have welcomed thee within the temple
  of my soul, have filled it with the beasts of passion or spent

my time in idle occupation with the vanities that pass, and
robbed thee of thy own.
And I—when thou didst live thy life so poor and meek to win
my love—
my life has been all comfort, ease, enjoyment;
and for praise and acclamation ever I have sought.

Thou wast subject to Joseph and thy blessed Mother,
and all thy life was to obey the Father's will;
and mine one long rebellion seeking self,
one long misuse of all thy grace.

Awaken thou my soul to follow all the way;
the crowded inn, the noise and tumult of the world,
refused thee birth.
Take thou my heart and enter in and drive without the passions
and the world; guide thou my worship and prepare a place
where thou mayest dwell, thy life my way; let nothing of my
own make void thy work, my God, my all.

DETACHMENT

*'He who aims at the attainment of God's love must needs confine all
his heart, mind, and energy for that single aim.'*
S. Francis de Sales, 'The Love of God,' xii, Chap. 3.

My God, my all,
draw thou my eyes from all but thee lest they behold
vanity; and quicken thou me in thy way.
All things created are but vanity unless they form the
footstool of thy throne.
My very soul is worse to me than any devil because it comes
between me and my God.
Grant me that vision of myself without which my soul may
never know thee,
my God, my all.
Grant me such light that each recess and corner of my soul
may be illumined, and grant the resolution that will
fear no pain, but grasp each wayward action and all that
is not sanctified for thee, that thou mayest take it thence.
Teach me to be alone with thee.

O God, why do I fear to be alone?
My treasure is all dissipated among the things of earth,
I crave for comfort from my fellow creatures, my interest is in the things that perish, my life is lukewarm, and sorrowfully I turn away when thou commandest me to follow thee alone.

O Lord, forgive. Let nothing hold my heart but only thee.

O soul, look well upon thy life.
What dost thou possess?
What canst thou do without?
What things are idols yet with thee?

Let nothing be possessed for its own sake or merit, for even the harmless doves in man-made cages were bidden to be taken forth from the Father's house.

O loving Saviour, who dost bid me leave all else save to endure thy cross and fellowship, grant me to follow thee,
thyself all stripped and emptied,
all for love of me,
myself all naked of all save thee;
clothe me with thy detachment from all save only thee.
The Father's will be done in me, as done in thee.
Grant me to know thee, O my Love;
to find in thee
the suffering of thy fellowship,
the rest of Love,
self lost in giving love and love's return.
Help me to die with thee, that I may for ever burn as one flame with thee. O God, my Love.

POVERTY

'*The immeasurable treasure of most holy poverty . . . this is that celestial virtue whereby all earthly things and fleeting are trodden under foot . . . this is the virtue that makes the soul, still tied to earth, hold converse with the angels in heaven, and this it is that hung with Christ upon the Cross, with Christ was buried, with Christ rose up again, with Christ ascended into heaven.*'
Little Flowers of S. Francis, Chap. xiii.

Possessing nothing, yet making many rich, thorn-crowned and reigning from the Tree, Love's wealth was bleeding wounds, stripes whence healing flows, a broken heart, an ever-springing fount of love that knows no end nor yet beginning, the Heart of God made manifest in human flesh, declaring all the riches of everlasting love.

Grant me, O Love, a share of this thy wealth, that having nothing of my own I may possess the virtue of thy wounds, my sins' forgiveness and a union with thy pain.

Thy riches no human wealth or toil may buy; freely thou givest to those who will accept nor count the cost of harbouring thy wealth of cross and shame that they may share thy joy.

Look well, O soul, within thy treasury.

Each thought and motive weigh, that no idol of thyself or of the world may claim thy heart, so that thy love may be his love, and so, returned in Love's own usury, the talents of thy soul may find fruition and increase according to the increase of his gifts.

It is the empty soul that learns the hunger of great love, even as the parched land in agony of dumbness waits the recreating rain by which the desert blossoms as the rose and all the plain is filled with life's new melody.

A great cry to my Love is emptiness, the hungering and thirsting shall be satisfied.

Revive, O Lord, within my soul the spring of Life, that from my nothingness may flow the living waters of thy peace—the gospel that thy slave in thee is free, free from all life's bitter bondage, the cares and tumults, selfishness and fierce idolatries that like ill weeds grow up and choke the grain thou sowest in the field.

Thy Life the seed, my soul the ground.

Thy Life the water whereby the seed may grow and bear its fruit.

Look well, O soul, art thou a road, a common haunt of other folk, a way wherein there is no rest but idle chatter of the crowd?

Hast thou dug deep and cleared the soil of all that lives beneath the outward semblance of thy life?

O soul, if thou wouldst be the ground wherein the Word may grow to fill thy life, consider well,

it was within the stable he was born
in deep humility.
The workshop knew his growing days,
in toil and service of his fellow men.
The perfect wheat was manifest in death.
Except a soul shall die it cannot live. Be nothing, O my
soul, have one desire to be *by* Jesus led, *with* Jesus on the
way, that *in* Jesus all shall be a life of dying, and a rest of
suffering, thy riches poverty and thy poverty abundant
wealth.
Too high, too hard this way
unless, my Jesus, thou art mine.

LOVE

'*Love wishes to tend upwards and is not to be held back by things
beneath. . . . If any man loves, he will know what is the utterance of
love.*'

Imitation, Book III, Chap. v. 3, 4.

Who may sing the song of Love?
Those only who give all, without reserve, hold nothing back,
'tis they who know the joy, the quickening pain of Love;
'tis they who taught by adoration hold the Heart of Love,
and touch all loveless hearts to life by giving Love.

From Love in Love the leaping flame of Love is spread,
for none can love except by Love possessed.
The love that is outpoured was first Love's gift of love.
Give, give, and give again
is Love's own song.
For Love is giving love and there is no end to Love.
Love is as the incense which giveth up its sweetness as it is
consumed.

Naked of all save love went Love, till naked in body,
wounded, pierced in agony of love,
Love broke the casket of the fount of love, that he might
draw all souls to find their end within the Heart of God.
Love waits so still,
for love must answer Love,
and we have wounded Love, betrayed, denied our Love.

Silent upon the Tree, made sin for us, Love waits that by the
     utmost gift of love, his broken Heart of Love, sin might
     no longer have dominion over us.

O loving Lord, thine eyes looked lovingly upon that woman in
     the hall, and at thy feet she wept in answering love:
     thine eyes searched Peter's face when thou wast ringed with
          scorn and enemies, and he went out and wept most bitterly
          in loving grief:
     upon the Cross in desolation's hour thy quiet gaze did draw
          the thief,
O Lord, remember me.

I have ringed thee round with hostility, denied thee.
I have sinned as rebel misusing all the gifts of life and
     love thou gavest me.
I have sinned by failing to respond to all thy perfect will
     for me.
Lord, give me love that I may know true penitence.

Lord, give me such desire for thyself alone:
     that I may hate myself,
     the self that wounds, scourges, nails, and crucifies thee still,
          that I may take each several power of my life and crucify
          the natural part of me, that all may be renewed, held fast
          in love.

Three nails may hold me fast to thee—
     obedience, dependence, reparation.
     Never to seek myself, but only walk love's way.
     Casting away all else, to possess love alone, and with love to
          share Love's giving of his love.

Prostrate before the feet of Love, Love's broken feet,
     two ways alone of life appear—
     to crucify him, or with him to be crucified.

Love's only song is giving, giving all.

How calm, majestical, Love walks life's paths;
     how sweetly calls his friends to come apart into the desert
     place:

'Be still and know,'
look out over God's harvest fields and pray.

Calm amid the storm he sleeps.
Love's power is of stillness born.

The fire of Love Divine is still.
  No flickering flame, the living movement of ever-rendered
    love.
  Hid deep within the mystery of the Unity,
    it burns a living darkness that is light,
    a light so pure that darkness is its flame.

O God, thou art the centre of my being, the homing-place of
  all desire, the universe of all and every love.

My Jesus, Light and Love, who showest me the inmost Heart
  of Love reigning upon the Tree, the sacred Heart, whose
  death wound was the Gate of Life.
  My Jesus, take thou thy dart and spear of love,
    pierce thou my heart that I may love, nor find a limit
  to my love.

Still, vibrant, giving, agonizing, is the soul of Love; its fruit
  more love, more pain, more longing, more desire, more
  souls for God, more sorrow, deeper penitence, a cry in all
  the world that thou, O God, art Love; and anguish that
  man's freedom turns from God; more souls, O God, more
  souls to love thee every day,

  O my God, if men did but know thee.

PURITY

*'As long as Jesus findeth not his image reformed in thee, he is
strange and far from thee. Shape thee, therefore, to be arrayed in his
likeness. . . .'*

                    Hilton, 'Scale of Perfection,' Book I, Chap. li.

The pure in heart, the single eye, alone shall see my God.
O God, thy Majesty abides so still, so far apart from my
  self-filled and wayward life.
O radiant Purity, that lives one fire, the fire of Love, consume
  me quite within thy quenchless flame.

O Virgin-born, true man, true God, may we possess thy love in purity, not for thy gifts or favours but for thyself alone, our all and every thought and wish and will thine everlasting glory.

My Lord, my King, how awful is thy presence in the sacramental veils, the Purity of God surrendered into human hands and human guardianship.

How dreadful is the place where on thy countless thrones faith hails thee present, or in dim unknowing thy Majesty is revered.

How clean the heart should be that welcomes thee its King: how pure the living house of prayer wherein thou wouldst abide.

How wonderfully thou didst form me that nothing but thyself may satisfy my soul's most inward longing.

My life is thine. Each day be then a gift to give to thee; a life to live for thee, to live thy Life, for thou didst give it me, and my life is thine.

O Love, to thee I do resign myself,
let nothing of my wretched self remain, but all of thee.

I do resign myself to bear whatever thou dost send;
to bear and to rejoice.

For love of thee, and in conformity to thy good will,
I now resign myself, if ever it may be thy will, to suffer shame and slander, unearned rebuke, to be forgotten of my friends, to want for food and natural comfort, to be abandoned and ignored by all my fellow men, so that I may have none to hold unto but only thee, my God; to suffer sickness and infirmity, to die alone in a strange land and among strangers, to endure aridity and pain of soul, to follow thee blindly, not seeking distraction or comfort in any creature, to be content to spend and to be spent for thee.

Take, O Lord, my freedom and my choice of things.

O Lord, thou gavest freedom to me that I might be freed from sin and from all that hampers me in returning thy love, my love to thee.

To thee, O Lord, I do return thy gifts; dispose of me according to thy will.

Let nothing cloud the mirror of my soul: may thy face alone illumine it.

Let nothing share the altar of my heart, lest strange fire, born of my unruled desire, burn thereon and cause thee to depart.

Burn thou alone within the temple thou didst fashion for thyself, and burning burn all dross of self away, so that thou mayest ever stay and never from my life depart; that in thy Purity I may obtain, the veil of flesh being rent by thee, my place before the Father's throne hid in thy Life within all Deity.

COURAGE

'*Above all the graces and gifts of the Holy Spirit which Christ has given to his friends, is that of conquering oneself, and suffering willingly for the love of Christ all pain, ill-usage, opprobrium, and calamity.*'

Little Flowers of S. Francis, Chap. vii.

O Love, O Purity,
    how may I come to find eternal rest in thee?
How may I bring with me the souls thou givest me to bring?
The seed must perish that new life may spring.
The wheat must die or ever it alone must stay.
O Jesus, thou art our guide:
    in thy life alone we life possess:
    teach us to die that we may live.
By the shadow of thy Cross upon thy cradle:
    by thine infant acceptance of the myrrh:
    by the words upon the mountain top
        that told of thy decease:
    by thy face set toward Jerusalem:
    by thy silence before thine accusers:
    by thy joyful acceptance of the Cross:
    by the awful stillness of thine Incarnate Life uplifted
        before the world of men:
                    pity our frailty.
Give us thyself
    that, nestling in thy broken Heart, we may endure with thee
    the agony of sinful man's return to holiness.
O Jesu, by thine awful penitence for us, bring us safely through those cleansing fires of Love, when hope seems dead and love can find no answer to its love, and faith is blind obedience bearing agony, and thou art not, and all is sin

and shame and loss, and nothing is, but horror of ourselves
and of the world and of the power of the air.
O God, in the hour of desolation grant us the faith to know
that thine absence from our consciousness is all our loss,
nor doubt that in the darkness thou art near.

Immortal Love, in man delivering man, lead on thy servant
by thy way from death to life:
set thou so clear before my eyes thy way of conquest that
I may never fear, but loving ever will to share the cost:
hold me so close that I may touch thy wounds and feel the
beating of thy Heart—
the very wounds I gave thee, O my Love,
the very Heart that broke for me,
the very wounds that conquered me and set me free
that I might love thee, O my Love,
the very Heart that, desolated, poured its love
to draw me in.
O Love, thy might is pain and desolation,
thy victory humiliation and life's outpouring.
O God, how sweet it is to serve thee in darkness and unknowing,
in contradiction and all undone, forlorn, bereft, alone.

'Tis faith that cleaves the darkness like a sword and cleaving
pierces him who wields.
'Tis hope that never can be satisfied till Love's most perfect
rest shall dawn.
'Tis love that here can know no rest, while sin and evil still
Christ's Body crucify.

The strength of love is faith,
the agony of love is hope.
O soul, be strong, be agonized, one life thou hast on earth
by which to give more love and yet more love to him who
loveth thee to such extremity.

Jesus, by thy love for men,
grant us thy servants strength that we may love them too,
so serving them we may serve thee and satisfy the hunger of
thy Heart.
O Love, if men did learn to love thee,
then all the world would know thy peace and thou wouldst
reign in every heart.

Make thou my hands and feet thy very own,
  let my heart be broken of thy pain,
  complete thy victory in this my soul
  that love may draw more souls to thee.
O Mystery of ever-loving Love, that love must give and love
  must share and never cease from loving toil, from Love in
  Love to Love, O loving God of Love.

CONCLUSION

'Therefore rest thee here, comfort thee here, live in Christ's heart
without end.'

> *A Meditation of the Five Wounds of Jesus Christ*
> *by an Early English Writer.*

Jesus, my Love, my King, my God, my friend, my life, my all,
  my only refuge and enduring hope, my Jesus.
To know thee, O my Love, be all my aim,
  in thee be lost, in thee be found.
My way thy way, my life thy life,
  that all the music of my soul be but one harmony, thyself.
O Mystery of Love unsearchable, that I the outcast *by* thee
  am lifted into life, *with* thee in sweetest intercourse may
  suffer here, enduring to the end, *in* thee may be fed with
  daily Bread, thy Life alone sufficing me.
O Love, give fear, that trembling in most holy dread I may
  receive thy love and never keep my own,
  and learn true love, for naught unloving may be found in
  thee.
Thy unity of love be all my care, and not one soul in all the
  world be absent from my prayer, so that the world may know
  thy love.
O Love, teach us to see the wounds that we have caused, the
  rents and tears, the schism and distress within thy Body
  here on earth, so that in penitence and self-forgetfulness in
  thee our prayer may be thy prayer; that all may be restored
  in thee, that through the world may be one song, one praise,
  one harmony with the eternal song of Love to Love in Love.
Praise and glory ever be
to Father, Son, and Holy Ghost,
Three Persons ever one:
Eternal Trinity.

Chapter VII

TO CALVARY: A MEDITATION

I

THE CONSIDERATION AND COMPOSITION OF PLACE

Calvary is not only a place and an occasion in history, but it is a spiritual reality in all times and places; for it is the at-one-ment of every soul to God.

It is in Calvary, the Blood-shedding of the Lamb, that Love in sacrifice draws out our love to answer his love to the fullest possibility of our sacrifice of self to him.

It is there that the soul can come to know its depth—of sin, of nothingness and of possibility for God.

It is there, face to face with Love in action, that the soul can learn to make answer to his love.

It is the meeting-place of lovers.

Pray therefore for the gift and increase of the three theological virtues—faith, hope, and charity—without which no soul can advance in the knowledge of God.

Saviour of bountiful mercy, Jesus most loving,
before thee I cast myself, contemplating in a soul filled with affection and grief the five wounds thou sufferest for me,
having before my eyes that which was said of thee in the psalm: 'They pierced my hands and my feet, I may tell all my bones';
I pray and beseech thee that through this contemplation of thy Passion
thou wouldest implant in my heart a full sense of faith, hope, and love,
true sorrow for my sins
and a firm resolve for amendment of life
with a steadfast purpose to follow thee only
my Saviour and my Lord.

II

LOVE SURRENDERS TO WIN LOVE

'. . . *Christ is still journeying whither he has gone before. For Christ went before us in the Head, and Christ follows in the Body. Christ is still here toiling; here Christ suffered at Saul's hands. . . . Christ is still here in want; here Christ still journeys; Christ here is sick, Christ is here in bonds.*'

S. Augustine, In Ps. lxxxvi. 5.

Jesus gives himself absolutely into men's hands that they may do with him what they will. His love is so great that he will do nothing to protect himself from men. As a lamb he is led to the slaughter, rejected by those whom he came to save.

The angel armies, wondering, watch, for it is his will: to win man's heart, he gives his own for man to break and pierce.

O my people, what have I done unto thee?
Behold and see if there be any sorrow like unto my sorrow.

Jesus, who, mocked, insulted, beaten, scorned, didst come
    to Calvary, have mercy upon us.
Jesus, scourged for our iniquities;
Jesus, unjustly condemned;
Jesus, betrayed and forsaken;
Jesus, delivered over to the will of thy enemies;
Jesus, patient in all suffering;
Jesus, by thy great love so manifested before the world,
    pour forth thy love upon thy world to-day.

O mystery of Love that Love must give so much.

O piteous wonder of thy Passion—
    that the Mother Maid who bore thee must tread upon thy
      sacred Blood all scattered on the way of earthly shame;
    that Magdalene at thy feet must mingle with the cleansing
      tide her tears.

O glorious wonder of thy Passion—
    that thy chosen ones and lovers may join with thee, and
      give thee comfort;
        thy pain is theirs, their suffering thine—

thy Mother's sword-pierced heart,
the penitent's bowed head,
the loving glance of him who leaned upon thy breast
in unquestioning surrender to thy will.

O Love, give love that love may never part from Love.

As on Calvary, so in his sacramental Presence, he surrenders himself absolutely into the hands of men; he is ours to love, welcome, and adore, or to reject, despise, take into a worldly and selfish heart, to wound in the house of his friends, to betray and to blaspheme.

Jesus, ever pleading at the heavenly throne, ever present in the
most holy Sacrament of the altar,
have pity in thy great love
on all who have misused thy precious Gift.
Jesus, sacred Victim, heaven on earth,
have pity in thy great love
on the careless and neglectful,
on those who forget thee present,
who receive thee unprepared, or dread to come to thee.
Jesus, in whose love all love that is love is found,
fill thy servant with such love, that in thee only shall
all his loves be found, thy life his life.
O Jesus, if men did but love thee, all would be well with them.
O Jesus, draw each one to love thee, by thy broken Body and
thy Blood outpoured, by the Cross of Calvary, by thy
Altar Throne.

III

LOVE TESTS HIS LOVERS

'*For only the servants of the Cross find the way of blessedness and of true light.*'

Imitation, Book III, Chap. xlvi. 2.

Jesus reigns from the Tree; on Calvary, in all the deep abasement of surrender to our human wills, he reigns as Saviour and as Judge.

'I came not to judge the world, but to save the world . . . the word that I have spoken, the same shall judge him that rejecteth me.' He reigns on Calvary to save those who recognize and accept the offered love, and hangs there the sorrowful witness and victim of our refusals.

By our attitude to Calvary we all are judged; we shall look on him whom we have pierced.

Jesus, pitiful Saviour, Judge most just, in the hour of our
    doom deliver us; give us such love to leave all else
    and seek thee only, as our end.

Jesus, nailed to the hard wood,
    mine the will that drove those nails;
Jesus stripped in the sight of men,
    mine the will that shamed thee so;
Jesus suffering the mocking jest, the bitter scorn,
    mine the thought that caused thee pain;
Jesus forgiving those who knew not what they did;
    I knew, and yet I wronged thee all the more;
by thy promise to the thief,
    forgive my reckless waste of all thy love;
by thy tenderness to those who loved thee,
    draw me to stand with them beneath thy Cross;
by thy thirst and agony,
    draw me to share the passion of thy love;
by the bitter cry of dereliction.
O human Saviour, suffering in thy creature's woe, forgive us
    when we leave thy side;
by the surrender of thy Spirit,
    forgive thy children's faltering faith;
by thy death,
    thy world restore.

Within the cleft of thy riven side hide us.
Keep us close within the broken heart of Love.
Break thou our hearts to fill us full of Love,
    for all the world must come to Calvary,
    and every road of life leads only to Golgotha;
    every soul that lives must stand before the Cross.
Two roads there are from Calvary:
    the straight way of heaven's gate is to share with
      thee the way.

O Jesus, hide me deep within thy riven side,
    for hell and endless torment ends that path that turns back-
        ward from the Cross.
O Jesus, hold thou me close to find the secret of thy broken
    heart.

Jesus comes in his sacramental Presence as Saviour, the
Life-giver, 'Except ye eat . . . ye have no life'; but also he
must come as Judge, for where he is there must be judgement:
in the words of an old Irish hymn on the Blessed Sacrament,

> *Alpha and Omega comes the Lord Christ,*
> *Comes his very self to judge the people.*

O Jesus, Judge and Saviour, spare;
Lord, we are not worthy that thou shouldest come under our
    roof:
    but if thou comest not, we die.
Have pity, Lord, in thy great love, on all who come to seek
    thy Presence and thy gift.
Come, Lord, in pity spare, in love make strong our hearts
    to bear thy Presence and thy love.
Burn with thy living fire the dross within our souls.
Thy fire of love make to fire our hearts,
    that other hearts may kindle at their glow,
    and thy love burn alone throughout the world,
    its all-sufficiency.

IV

LOVE THIRSTS FOR LOVE

'*I understood that we be now . . . . in his Cross with him in his pains*
and his Passion, dying; and we willingly abiding in the same Cross
with his help and his grace unto the last point, suddenly he shall change
his cheer [i.e. *countenance*] *to us, and we shall be with him in heaven.*'
            Julian of Norwich, 'Revelations of Divine Love,' Chap. xxi.

Calvary reaches out to the very limits of human being, to
the very bounds of creation. The Cross upholds in time the
timeless Word without whom was not anything made that was
made. He in creation so enters into our being that nothing is
done that does not touch him, and to restore us to the fullness

G

of life, he has gathered all humanity, all suffering, and all love
to himself as Man on Calvary.

From all fear and dread of thy Cross,
from all selfishness and hardness of heart,
from all impurity and deadly sin that would hurt thee in us,
from pride and self-sufficiency,
from the deceits of the world, the flesh, and the devil,
    good, loving Lord, deliver us.

O Jesus, suffering in the world of men,
    give us the single eye to see thee plain;
    for blind with sin and self are those who see thee not,
    as the Cross stands amid the suffering world to-day.

        Hail, holy Cross, life-giving Tree,
            our only hope,
            and our most bitter shame.
        Hail, holy Cross, which bears the living Lord.

O Jesus, we have wounded thee, and shamed thee so many
    times and knew it not;
    carelessly and wantonly often we have put self first and
      wronged thee in thy children;
    we have passed thee by in the sinner and the sufferer, the
      stranger and the needy;
    no cup of water have we given thee,
    no thought or prayer to share thy anguish,
    no visit to declare our love,
    no sympathy to support the desolate,
    no tear mingled with the tears of those that weep.

O Jesus, my sharp word and unkind deed against my brother
    man was a stone cast at thee on the road to Calvary's hill.
O Jesus, my foul speech and filthy thought
    was my treading underfoot the Precious Blood upon the
      way of sorrow.
O Jesus, my common share in corporate wrong
    is joining in the crowd who cry, 'Crucify him, crucify.'

O Jesus, pity me, give me love to love thee;
    so poor my penitence,

so grudgingly thy love returned,
that dry-eyed I sit and watch thee
nor fear to sin again.

O Jesus, by thy bands of love
draw thou me to thy Cross and bind me there,
lest I waste all and cause thee further pain.

Tremble, my soul,
for I have nailed my Love upon the Cross.
Tremble, O my soul,
for I have crucified my Lord,
by unkind word,
by cruel deed,
by evil thought,
nor seen thee suffering in my fellow men,
nor run to love thee when thou gavest opportunity.

See now, O soul, the tumult,
hear now the uproar and the shouting,
Love is led out to die by those he loved;
Love is stripped naked in the sight of men,
showing the wounds he suffered for the sake of men;
Love is nailed through hands and feet,
on the Cross with body racked and drained of blood.

Love reigns lifted above the world of men—
darkness above, the trembling earth beneath.
'I thirst,' Love cries,
and all the world is thirsting in that cry.
'I thirst for love,' Love cries:
'give me thy love, that thou mayest share my thirst.'

V

LOVE SHOWS THE WAY OF LOVE

'Many follow Jesus as far as the breaking of bread, but few to the drinking of the cup of his Passion.'

Imitation, Book II, Chap. xi. 1.

The soul that would find Love, true Love, must come to Calvary and enter the darkness of the Passion. Love's meeting-place is hid within the living darkness, dark night that hides from this world's passing day the splendour of the everlasting light of Love. He who will not deny himself, nor mortify his will and inclinations, but would seek the treasure of Love at ease and without cost, will never find; and if such as he should stand on Calvary it will not be with the lovers that he will find his place, but with the curious, the idle watchers, and the foes.

O soul that wouldst seek Love on Calvary, look close within thyself, see clear the ground thou standest on, the company thou holdest with.

Look well, O soul, as thou comest to Calvary.
Art thou amid the careless crowd that mocked Love there,
    or weepest thou apart,
    or, gaining courage from thy love,
    art thou with those who following close are standing by
      his side?
Is thy heart racked, as Mary's heart was racked, by every
    ribald jest, stunned by each wanton blow, and lacerated
    by the wounds he bears?

O Love that ever suffers in thy world of men,
    give us the strength to bear with thee some pain.

O Mystery of Love, that love must give so much.

O Saviour, give us thy strength that we may never part from
    thee, whate'er befall;
    come suffering, pain, or dread, Lord Jesus, give us love
    to cast out fear.

O Jesus, hide me deep within thy riven side,
    for hell and endless torment ends the way that turneth
    backward from the Cross.
O Jesus, hold thou me close to find the secret of thy broken
    heart.
O soul, consider well thy way—
    whose likeness seest thou as thine in all that throng?
See there the frenzied mob that with instant voice did make a
    mock of justice, crying 'Crucify.'

See the cruel soldiery that scourged and drove thy Lord unto the place of death.

See the jealous scribe, and bitter Pharisee, the mocking priest, and proud contemptuous ruler.

O soul, look well, there stand religious men who by their law condemned their God to die, and business men who feared his influence on their profit.

O Love Incarnate, bleeding for thy human race,
    have pity, spare;
    not once but many times for God's own Name have martyrs bled,
    not once but many times has wealth condemned the innocent.

O Cross, my only hope, my wretchedness befriending, let others bind me to the wood, so that at last I nevermore can go from thee, my Love.

VI

RESOLUTION AND OFFERING

Love waits on Calvary for our love to answer his. If we are to find the fullest meaning of our faith, it will be in the study of the mystery of redemption. If we are to make our prayer more real, it will be by facing Love, crucified by human sin, to show him our wretched sinfulness in penitence and to plead with him for his sinning and suffering children.

At Calvary there can be no suppression or hiding away our shortcomings and vices; they crucify him. At Calvary, for his sake, all souls must be loved and borne with, patiently and lovingly.

Resolve therefore to meditate often and long upon Christ's Passion and his suffering love. He will never let us go if we really want to stay with him; but we must perform our part by filling our understanding and memory with thoughts of the meeting-place of lovers, and setting our hearts upon it. So we may bring its reality to bear upon the passing circumstances of the world in which we are called to live and work for him.

O soul, look well
    and count the cost of love,
    lest thou thy pilgrimage begin
    and lacking love may perish by the way,
    for love alone can reach to love
    and reaching bear the judgement of Love's fire.

Love by love alone is perfect made,
    for love is living out in love the call of Love,
    for love is in exchange of love
    resolved in will and signified by deed;
    for deed without will is loveless act,
    and will without deed falls short,
    to die stillborn through sinful negligence
        and lack of love's exchange.

        Lord, give me love.

O Love, that came to cast the living fire on earth
    inflame the souls that love thee much
        to burn with brighter light;
    inflame the souls that love so timidly
        that they may love thee more;
    set thou on fire the souls that love thee not
        that they may answer love by love.

O Love, my God, my Jesus, I would come to thee, I have no
    strength to come, draw me from all my evil ways,
    that freely I may come and clasp the living Cross,
    that freely I may give myself to be thy servant and thy
    loving friend.
    So may I dwell on Calvary, with Mary stand and with
        Magdalene weep, nor ever leave thy side.

O loving Saviour, give thou the strength of love to stay by thee
    in fear, in darkness, loneliness, and pain, if such be thy will.
Lord Jesus, give us thy love to trust and hold thee close when
    nothing shows thee near.
Lord Jesus, give us thy love to see all men in thee and thee in
    all.
        O Love, O God, O Life.
        O God my All.

CHAPTER VIII

FELLOWSHIP IN SUFFERING

A MEDITATION WITH COLLOQUIES

I

PREPARATION

It is meet for us to glory in the Cross
       of our Lord Jesus Christ:
         in whom is our salvation,
         our life and our resurrection.
Thy Cross, O Lord, we adore
       and we contemplate thy glorious passion
         by which we are saved and made free.

We pray thee, O Christ, that by the contemplation of thy
Cross and Passion we may ever be strengthened to do
thy will, so that we may at length behold the clear
vision of thy Face where thou reignest with the Father and
the Holy Spirit, ever one God, world without end. Amen.

II

*'God so loved the world, that he gave his only-begotten Son, that
whosoever believeth in him should not perish, but have everlasting life.'*
                           S. John iii. 16.

God so loved the world,
       the world that loves him not,
       the suffering world of pain and death and separation,
       of vice and cruelty and selfishness
         that lies within the power of the evil one,
     that unto it he gave his only Son
       to be the full, perfect and sufficient sacrifice,
       oblation and satisfaction
     for the sins of the whole world.

God gives, and I must give
    my love to answer love, in love's dependence.
  'I acknowledge my faults: and my sin is ever before me':
    have mercy, Lord, forgive.

God gave in plenitude of love
    the one and only perfect offering,
    his very self, offered once for all,
    gathering into Love's oblation the fullness of all created
      being:
    sinless made to be sin:
    to know and suffer sin without the guilt of sin:
    through death destroying death:
    in resurrection making unity and peace,
    himself the fullness that filleth all in all.

God gives, and I must give
    my love to answer Love, in loving penitence.
'Make me a clean heart, O God: and renew a right spirit
    within me':
    have mercy, Lord, that I may be restored to life in thee.

God gave, and giving took the servant's form of our humanity
    to make complete and perfect unity of God and man in love:
    to suffer every pain of separation:
      in spirit desolate
      in blood outpoured
      in body broken
      in agony of death
      in grief at man's refusal and ingratitude:
   that in his sinlessness made perfect
     humanity in him might have no sin;
   that in his unity and through his grace
     man's life should be restored to know the Father
     and receive the Spirit in the Trinity;
   that living as the branches in the Vine
     men should bear the fruit of the Vine to life eternal,
     in filling up the sufferings that remain,
     as time succeeds to time,
     until the consummation of the end.

God gives, and I must give
    my love to answer love, in loving confidence.
'The sacrifice of God is a troubled spirit; a broken
    and a contrite heart, O God, shalt thou not despise':
have mercy, Lord, grant me thy peace
    whereby I know I dwell in thee and thou in me.

        My Love is crucified.
          He holds us in his Cross,
          and in his hands
            there is life:
            in the midst of death, confidence:
            in the midst of suffering, peace
              that passeth understanding.

        My Love is crucified.
          He reigns from the Tree
          gathering his saints in every age
            their sufferings his
            his sufferings theirs
            in love's exchange
          to manifest unto the world
          his Way, his Truth, his Life.

God gave himself, abandoning all save love
    in suffering sacrifice to overcome the separation
        of self-love and lovelessness.
        Naked of all save love,
        Love takes into the exchange of love
        the burden and result of lovelessness.
        Naked of all save love,
        Love clothes himself in suffering
        to expiate the cruelties and wrongs,
        the conflicts and the desolations
            of self-love.

God gives, and I must give
    a life that knows the pain of separation
    a life which is informed and led by penitence,
    in penance and in service
    to recover unity.

O Lord forgive the selfishness that would maintain
    my self-sufficiency,
        that dreads to give the service which thou dost command,
        to love and serve as thou dost love and serve.

O Lord forgive, wash thou my feet
    that I may follow close
    nor leave thee
    when the world and men condemn.

O Lord forgive, feed thou my soul,
    that drawn within thy life,
    thy life in me may overcome the weakness of
        my fallen state
    and hold me safe from all the manifold temptations of
        the fiend.

God gave
    that in all ages
    believing souls might pass from perishing to life—
    to know him
    and the power of his resurrection,
    learning through fellowship in his sufferings,
    conformed unto his saving death.
    No man can serve two masters.
    God's gift of life is man's to take
            or to refuse.

God gives, and I must give in love to answer love,
    that I may be bound fast within the tree of life
        to bear his fruit.

O Lord forgive my little effort to make dead
    my own concupiscence that wastes my life
    and hinders thee to form the fruit that thou wouldst find.

O Lord forgive, lest fruitless I remain, and when
    thou comest thou shalt find the tree barren.

O Lord forgive; take thou my hands and feet
    and bind them to thy Cross

that I may live with thee
and work with thee thy work
in drawing all that is not love
to Love *in* love *by* love;
in dying to myself
in suffering and in living unto thee
for those who love thee not.

My Love is crucified.
He came unto his own.
Men pass him by.
He reigns as judge on Calvary,
    the place of love's exchange
    where men still crucify,
    by act or by neglect,
or come to stand within the circle of his friends—
to learn to share his saving pain.

O Lord forgive; I cannot love as I would love;
    take thou my love, my life, and make it thine,
                Jesus, my Jesus.

Jesu, mercy.
    Sinless, all sin is gathered up in thee,
    that love may expiate the guilt
    and satisfy the punishment that separates the soul from life.

Jesu, mercy.
    The world is full of sin and pain and cruelty.
    We pass it by, seeking out comfort and avoiding suffering;
    Our sins have wounded thee,
    Our sins and selfishness make us draw back
        when thou dost call—
            'Take up thy cross and follow me.'

O Lord forgive the disobedience of the human will
    that sought its own, refusing love's exchange of liberty,
    and justly found itself condemned to death.

O Lord forgive the men who pass thee by—
    who do not see the damning judgement of their guilt

nor feel the horror of their sin,
that thou, our God in human life, shouldst die through
sin,
a costly recompense that man might live.

O Lord forgive: wound thou my heart
that I may know increasingly
thy sorrow for the sins of men,
and dread lest I may wound or pass thee by.

My Love is crucified.
How few will stand beneath the Cross.
He reigns to draw all hearts
to know the bitterness of sinful self-fullness;
to find the life of selflessness
in love's exchange.

Spirit of God, most holy Paraclete,
dwelling within the Church,
by whom the saints do speak,
proceeding from the Father and the Son,
make clear our sight
that we may see and know
how separateness must find itself again in unity
by separate and unique response of will;
creature to Creator answering,
yet bound by common nature each to all
to spend itself in service each for each,
each life a leaf within the book of life,
in Adam dying and in Christ alive.

The Church is one, holy and complete, and yet completing
Christ's very Body, and his Bride,
wherein all things created
are brought into subjection to their source and end,
the Word of Life.

The Church is one in essence indivisible:
on earth in mode and continuity of passing time,
in suffering as the days succeed to days:
in glory waiting for the consummation of the end
in modeless unity.

The Church on earth
    must watch and wait the fullness of the glory yet to be.
    The shadow of the Cross lies over it,
    the power of the Cross sustains it
      in suffering's fellowship.
    The Cross is on the altar,
    the Cross is on the spire:
      we must not sleep
      if one with Christ we are to live.

III

'*When they were come to the place which is called Calvary there they crucified him.*'

S. Luke xxiii. 33.

To Calvary
    all roads on earth must come,
    for man doth ever injure man through sin
    until the end of time.
    Christ's pain is manifest.
    We must not sleep if we are one with him.

The Lord of life,
    he came to Calvary
    bending his will upon the Father's love—
    'Not my will but thine be done'—
    accepting nature's bondage and the cost of sin
    to make all free within the heart of Love,
      the living Way of Truth,
    that we, through love's response, by giving love
      to answer Love's request
      by suffering taught
        by him
        in him
        with him
      might find his peace,
        the cheerful vision of his face,
      and live with him
        in him
        by him
      in Love's eternal flow and pulse of love,
        from death made free

from sin redeemed
in life restored,
to know in him
the eternal majesty of Love
in Trinity and Unity.

Love's victory is made complete in Calvary,
yet is the pain prolonged till sin be done away.
We must not sleep if we would be in unity with him,
our Saviour and our Friend.

My Love is crucified.
The Cross is on the altar,
the Cross is on the spire,
and men pass it by:
Love's pain is man's neglect.

Jesus, my Lord, my God, my Saviour, and my all:
forgive the world's neglect
and my forgetfulness.

Thou callest us:
'take up thy cross and follow me.'
Not from the world thou callest us
but to the world in love thou sendest us,
kept from the evil if in thy Cross we live and die,
that men may know thou lovest them.

IV

'Father, forgive them; for they know not what they do.'
S. *Luke* xxiii. 34.

Thou callest:
The men who sent thee there
thought they did God good service.
The unthinking, mocking soldiery who scourged
and crowned and nailed thee,
obeyed the law's command.
Thy friends, the army of thy kingdom
all but a few, a very few, had fled.
The busy world passed by, or paused a moment
to watch a criminal led out to die.

My Love is crucified.
    The Church on earth is rent by grievous wounds,
    men doubt its faith,
    scorn its virtues,
    repudiate its laws.

My Love is crucified.
    Man sets himself supreme
    by knowledge seeking to control the natural
    and to condition men to human ends.

O Lord make haste
    to show the way
    whereby in faith and penitence
    through prayer and suffering
    thy Church may live in unity restored
    to preach thy Gospel that men may live.

And I, what hinders my amendment?
    It is myself,
    my care for self,
    my self-importance in the scheme of things:
I would protect and guard myself
I would give rein to my creative life,
    each separate passion striving to attain its
        proper satisfaction:
    the wounds I feel I would repay,
    the pains I feel I would relieve:
I cannot pray for those who injure me—Forgive.

Saviour, patient, strong, and kind,
    break my hard soul
    that cannot reach thee,
    that cannot touch thee,
    that fears and dreads thee
    and yet doth love thee.

        Thou callest—
        Dare we come?

V

'Lord, remember me when thou comest into thy kingdom.'
S. Luke xxiii. 42.

Thou callest,
> not in the secret places of the earth
> but in the market,
> in the town, in daily tasks,
> in being true to love
> and love's forgiveness,
> upon the hill where thou art crucified before the face of
> men.

I set thy wounds before my face.
> By feet and hands,
> the Shepherd's feet that sought the lost,
> the hands that healed the sick,
> by wounded side and thorn-crowned brow,

I pray to thee—forgive.
> Most justly we do suffer,
>   for the sin of man is plain;
>   only thou art innocent.

My Lord, my Saviour, and my God,
> remember me
> that I may live and die in thee.

>   My Love is crucified.
>   The nails are in thy hands,
>   the thorns are on thy brow,
>   men pass thee by
>   with murmurings and tumult of desire,
>   with clamour of activity that will not stay
>   or heed the truth
>   that love must suffer to redeem.

VI

'Now there stood by the Cross of Jesus his Mother.'
S. John xix. 25.

>   I would kneel before thy Cross
>   and kiss thy wounds.

Lift thou me up
   to bear thy grief.

Mary, Mother,
   was there no other way?
   The Lord of life chose this:
   to hold all sin and death,
     all time and circumstance
   in Love's embrace
   upon the Cross,
   nailed fast in stillness,
     for love must give nor count the cost.

John, disciple who learnt best
   that love is giving in response to love—
     'We love because he first loved us'—
   whose love, dependent and obedient, held him fast
     beside the Cross,
   who would not leave till he was told
     to take the Mother home,
     and then returned.

John, most faithful in thy love,
   is there no other way?
   Must Love endure,
   ignored and hated,
     while men pass by?

   Love will not force the human will
     that it created free.
   Love will endure by activity of love proved in love's
     suffering,
   and draw and draw until the end.

Saviour, pity, break, and take me:
   break my bondage,
   my self-complacency,
   all that comes betwixt us ;
   all that makes me
   fear and dread thee;
   for I love thee,
   and would give thee all thou askest:
   draw me close and closer to thee.

H

Three nails held Love on Calvary
  and witnessed to the cost of sin;
  blood-stained and heavy,
  bent from the hammer's blow,
    each blow a pain.
Three virtues strong held Love
  and hold the Body of his Church
    on Calvary.
Three virtues strong,
  faith, hope, and charity,
  to hold me close in Love's embrace
  and make me one with him.

Mary, Mother,
  must love endure,
  not only once but to the end of time,
  while men pass by?

Beside the Cross our Lady Mary stood:
  she knew the bitterness of that still fastening,
  the crippling bondage of time and circumstance,
  the cost of sin and death:
    faith's agony
    hope's desolation
    love's victory.

She knew, her heart transfixed beside the Cross,
  faith stretched to love's attainment,
  hope resolved in love's fruition,
  love, everlasting love, in Love's completeness,
    triumphant over death in Calvary.

She knelt at Bethlehem:
  faith's adoration hailed the King,
  her Child and Saviour,
  earth's Redeemer, Heaven's Lord.

She lay beside the tomb,
  her soul all desolate for sin's apparent victory
  though hope still burned
  a living flame,
  'despite this cost can God his people fail?'

She wept in woeful isolation—
   a loving heart its love can never lose—
   nor understood the why.
   Yet love proclaims insistent
     'Be it unto me according to thy word.'
   'He is not less my child within the tomb
     nor less my God than he proclaimed himself to be.'

She knew the joy that Easter brought,
   wherein faith found its goal in sight
   and hope was satisfied in love's embrace.

She knows—our Lady Mary, Queen of Heaven,
   Mother of her Lord and ours—
   the long-drawn patience of the war
   that the Church, the Body of her Son,
   must wage till time be done.

Mary, our Mother,
   three nails held thee,
   three gifts of grace,
     faith, hope, and charity;
   pray thou for us
   that in the Cross our souls may learn,
     nailed fast,
   Love's endless gift of love
     unvanquished through the cost of sin and death.

Mary, Mother,
   aid my prayer
   that I may learn from him, thy Son our Lord,
     and stand with thee beside the Cross,
     held fast in faith and hope and charity.

This day of time, in which I breathe the breath
   of my mortality,
   becomes for me through Calvary
   a moment of eternity,
   the door to immortality,
   if to the Cross I give myself
     to walk by faith:

if by the Cross I make my stand
  to suffer hope:
if in the Cross I give myself to him
  to bear in love what he shall will.

Saviour, patient, strong, and kind,
    in life, in death,
    in health, in sickness,
    in pain, in joy,
    in pleasantness and in discomfort,
    in loneliness and in union,
    in every breath I breathe and thought I think,
    in time and in eternity,
      draw me to thee.

Thou callest.
  Dare we come?
I would kneel me down beneath thy Cross
  and kiss thy feet.
Lift thou me up
  and fold me in thy love.

VII

'My God, my God, why hast thou forsaken me?'
                                   S. Mark xv. 34.

My Love is crucified.
  We must not sleep when all is dark
  when every effort seems to fail
    and love elicits no response from love.

On Calvary
    all sin, all that falls short of God's full purpose,
    is gathered in the broken heart of Love's own prayer
      to make rebellion recognize defeat,
      to bring to separation unity.
    Love's soul is desolate
      as a diver penetrates the deep to win the pearl,
      so sinless Love is deep engulfed in sin.

On Calvary
    where love and sin are made at one:
    there Christ is made all sin for us
      and sinless bears the cost of sin,
    that he, in meek obedience to the law of death,
    might break for ever
      the chain of necessary effects,
      renewed by sin through sin,
    till self itself accepts the task of selflessness
      and love is all.

On Calvary
    the Word of God in flesh,
    through mortal death, death's penalty destroyed
    and offered in one moment, once for all,
    the wholeness of created time and space
    in his created body of our mortality,
      by him in him immortalized.

On Calvary
    God's very self and sin's denial of the Majesty of God
      joined final battle.
    Obedience and disobedience held in one embrace of love
    whereby the infinite compassion of God's love,
      absolute in mercy,
      just and free,
    bound once for all the finite hate
      wherein self-will abides alone
      in restless struggle for its own sufficiency
      in torment of destruction and of accusation
      making hell.

        My Love is crucified.
          It is the hour of darkness;
          to-day the lights are dimmed,
          iniquity abounds,
          the love of many waxes cold.

        My Love is crucified,
          wounded in the house of his friends,
          neglected by the multitude.

His Church, his Body on earth, divided,
while few care and fewer give themselves
to penance for their sin:
his saving Cross
to Jew a stumbling-block,
to Greek a foolishness,
is thought no longer pertinent to preach.

My Love is crucified.
        The Cross is on the altar:
            few come to it.
        The Cross is on the spire:
            the many pass it by.

O Lord, how long
    shall easier gospels take the place of truth
    while faith gives place to acquisition of
        immediate gains
    and hope of final victory is lost in hope for
        lesser things
                as love grows cold?

O Lord, forgive,
    it is an hour of darkness.
    While man's sufficiency becomes the measure of
        mankind
    men doubt and seek their own
        in the dark places of the earth,
        in habitations of cruelty
        where liberty of choice is lost,
            directed by conditioning,
        and violence rules,
                and the exploited earth grows barren.

My Love is crucified.
        Shall he find faith
            if he come again?
        Are there no eyes to see the gospel life
            and follow it?
        The Way that overcomes in fellowship of suffering,
        the Truth that nothing can refute,
        the Life still crucified.

The Cross is on the altar:
　　he cometh to his own.
The Cross is on the spire:
　　the many pass it by.

　　Love gives nor counts the cost
　　　　for love is giving
　　　　freely giving
　　　　giving all.

God freely gives, for freedom is God's own attribute;
　　only the Uncreated can be truly free.
　　That which has origin is bound to its own origin
　　　　within the terms of its particular createdness.
　　Man's freedom is of God;
　　　　from God alone is knowledge of true liberty
　　　　in worship and dependence made effectual,
　　　　　　love giving in return to Love.

　　All that neglects, that passes by the Gospel of the Cross
　　　　unheeding, crucifies:
　　all that despises the way of gentleness and self-oblation
　　　　for the sake of others, crucifies:
　　all that persecutes and sacrifices common good
　　　　for self-advancement, crucifies.

　My Love is crucified:
　　how cold my heart, so full of my own fears:
　　how slow my mind to understand the meaning of apostasy,
　　　　that man will choose Barabbas still
　　　　and Caesar's approbation still prevails:
　　how weak my will to give myself to stand beneath the
　　　　Cross and share his pain.

　　　　Thou callest.
　　　　　　The Cross is on the altar.
　　　　Dare we come in desolation's hour
　　　　　　to bear thy grief?

　　　　Thou callest.
　　　　　　The Cross is on the spire.

Dare we come in desolation's hour?
    Thou leadest us without the gate
    to witness in a world of men
        that loves thee not
        and passes by.

'Lord I believe, help thou my unbelief.'
    So spake the loving parent of the deaf and dumb,
        possessed by Satan's power,
    and thou didst heal.
Touch my deaf ears that I may hear the myriad sorrows
    of the sons of men
        nor dull my senses by the sounds of my own cares.
Restore my sight that I may see thy world as thou dost see.
Inflame my love, make free my soul
    that I may go with thee
    and bear with thee all that thou wilt choose for me
    for as long as thou dost choose.

VIII

'*I thirst.*'
S. John xix. 28.

God thirsts and man must thirst with God
    if he would come to know the heart of God;
    a very thirst in which the body's discipline must teach
    the soul to taste of death and sin's confusion.

God thirsts and man must thirst with God,
    that by a death to self he may a worthy worship give:
    a thirst that knows no rest till man returns
    the love that first did love, and formed humanity.

God thirsts and man must thirst with God
    if he would overcome the vanities that pass,
    and know the rest of energy eternal
    hid in the overflowing depths of Love's unchanging heart.

Teach me, my Lord, to thirst in deed,
    to see my sloth, my own self-fullness,
    all that holds my heart and will,
    all that keeps my soul imprisoned from thy liberty.

Teach me, my Lord, to feel the need of souls,
    that I may bear them up to thee in prayer,
    nor fail thee in the bearing.

Teach me, my Lord, to follow faithfully thy way for me,
    nor try to alter it for any thought of mine—
    for any pressure from the world of men.

Teach me, my Lord, to know when I must give
    through hand or word or prayer
    a ministry to thee in other men.

Teach me, my Lord, a pure intent of loving thee,
    that all my will may tend to the eternal end
    where thou alone art now the all-in-all.

Thy lips pronounce the hunger of thy soul
    and body's pain in penance for the sins of men.
    A thirst for mine and all men's love
    unquenchable until the consummation of the end.

                Thou callest.
                Dare we come?

        I would stand beneath the Cross
           to live with thee.
        Touch thou my lips
           to feel thy thirst,
           that I may thirst with thirst insatiable,
       a thirst unquenchable till unity is known
           between my soul and thee;
       a thirst unquenchable while ought remain
           unloving in the face of Love,
           unreconciled before the passion of thy sacrifice.

God thirsts and I with Love must thirst
    if I would come to know the heart of Love
    or reach unto the lips of Love.

Love made the bridge that spans the river of the perishing,
    the living bridge, from death to life,
    of Love's own crucifixion.

Lord, give me grace to walk that bridge
   through gate of penitence and holy fear,
   by way of close attention to thy will
   and knowledge of thy heart's desire,
   unto the crown and end:
   to give the fullness of my life
   in love's oblation:
   to work with thee thy work of liberation.

Lord, give me grace
   to walk in order,
   grace succeeding grace accepted,
   lest by desire of myself or Satan's guile
   I wilfully draw back in servile fear
   or wilfully press on and fail because of pride.

Lord and loving Saviour, Shepherd of thy sheep,
   grant that my way by thee be ordered
   that I may walk and follow thee
   solely as thou willest and dost give me grace.

   Thou who gavest thyself wholly for me
   teach me to give myself wholly to thee.

IX

'It is finished.'
St. John xix. 30.

Lord, I believe that thou hast set all things beneath thy feet:
   that thy work is finished indeed,
   no evil left unredeemed.
     My Love is crucified.
      We must not sleep
      for he has conquered death
      to give man life.
   No hope is now too high
   no love impossible if thou shouldst will it,
   and if man wills to pay the cost
   in union with thy love,

in prayer and discipline
in oneness with thy purpose of reconciliation,
accomplished and displayed in crucifixion.

    O Lord forgive
        the weakness of my soul that knows
        that thou hast conquered
        and yet fears to give itself to thee
        to be made clean and wholly one with thee.

My Lord, my God
        ringed with enemies, despised, rejected, scorned,
        by friend deserted,
        lonely,
        in solitary separation lifted on the Tree,
        exposed before the multitude that passed by,
        between two thieves
        in darkness:
        after long silence and endurance
        thou didst speak the word:
        'It is finished.'

    O Lord forgive
        the weakness of my soul that dreads
        the loneliness of victory.

        Thou callest.
           Dare we come
           to share with thee
           thy victory?

Christ, himself the living gospel, spake the word of triumph:
        'It is finished.'
    In him one full humanity was reconciled to God,
    in him all human walls of separation were broken down
        made one in death:
   as Adam dies, the life of Christ is made alive.
     The old is past,
     the veil is rent,
     that in each heart of man a brighter shrine
     should be prepared of spirit and in truth
     to be a living temple of the Holy Ghost.

'It is finished.'
>By sacrifice the creaturely dependence that was bound
>>in sinful separation
>is returned to liberty.
>By suffering all the pain of love refused
>>was by Love's will renewed within Christ's broken heart.
>By love man's will created free, to give its love in full return,
>>is brought to love again,
>is drawn to lose its life in penitential death,
>>to find its life and liberty reborn in Christ alone.

The soul, baptized, regenerate in the Body of the Lord,
>is free, yet not its own to act licentiously.
Christ healed it by his blood outpoured:
Christ bought it with a bitter price:
Christ claims it by a living word:
>'It is finished.'
>Adam is dead, Christ's bondslave lives.

The soul fresh cleansed by absolution's gift
>>hears once again that piercing cry:
>'It is finished.'
>It learns afresh the merits of the precious blood;
>in penitence it rises free,
>by penitence to express
>the knowledge of its fall.

Christ spake the word:
Christ gave the life:
>>and yet
>man's liberty to sin maintains the past,
>and progress mocks the world's complacency
>in multiplying new destructiveness,
>new wars, new torments,
>new exploitations, new oppressions,
>new deserts following hard behind man's plough,
>and birth itself refrains to give new life
>and is restrained by human will,
>>and yet
>Christ reigns from the Tree.

I gaze on thy Cross,
  O Saviour suffering for my love:
  was ever love like thine
  or sin like mine?

I gaze on thee crucified,
  O Saviour suffering for my love :
  take me to thyself,
  keep me in thy wounds,
  ever to love thee, in pain and in bliss,
  in earth and in heaven
  with thee for ever.

My Love is crucified.
  Love will not force the human will
    created as the mirror of God's loveliness
    for love's return.
  Love waits on Calvary to draw assent from willing souls:
  Love waits in suffering and in contradiction,
    to win response by offering love that love may be
    returned.

Love waits in agony of love refused,
  a pain which is not limitation of love's force
  but love's increase.
Love's voice rings down the ages from the Cross
  till all be finished and complete.

My Love is crucified.
  Eternally he pleads his one sufficient sacrifice
    in marks of scourge and thorns
      of nails and spear:
    the very wounds that Thomas reached to touch,
    and fell before his wounded feet and cried,
      'My Lord, my God.'

My Love is crucified.
  His victory won, the darkness passes.
  We may not sleep, the day is here.
  His work in us, through us, is now begun—
    to spread the knowledge of the Gospel light;
    to make effectual in every age and place
    Love's victory over sin and death.

The Cross is on the altar:
   the nails are in thy hands.
The Cross is on the spire:
   the thorns are on thy brow.

Are there no hands to be outstretched in prayer,
   nailed to thy Cross,
   enduring to the end that day may come?
Are there no feet to hasten on thy way,
   to find the sheep that are lost—to bind the wounds
     of stricken men,
   spending and being spent for thee?
Are there no eyes to see beneath the thorns of pain
   thy grief that men pass by—
   to see that thy people love to have it so?

Most blessed Lord, still suffering for our sake within thy
   Church, forgive:
By pierced hands
   by broken feet
   by bleeding brow
O Lord we pray,
   inflame thy Church, inflame the souls
     that call thee Lord,
   that in this time of faithlessness and doubt
   a new apostolate of prayer and sacrifice
     may manifest thy love
   in victory over sin and death,
   may prove thy word victorious,
      'It is finished'
   enduring to the end.

Most blessed Lord, forgive the coldness of thy Church,
   its preoccupation with the things that pass,
     with privilege and wealth,
     security and worldly power.
Most blessed Lord, forgive the lukewarm souls
   who cling to ease and comfort
     and refuse thy call unto discipleship;
   who count the cost, yet call thee 'Lord,'
     wounding thee within the household of thy friends.

My Lord, my God, my Love, my King,
>> thou gavest all for me:
>>> the wounds are in thy hands
>>> the thorns are on thy brow
>> bring me to give my all to thee
>>> my thoughts, my time, my energy, my doing
>>>> and my rest.

>>> Thou callest.
>>>> Needs must we come,
>>>> my Lord, my God.

x

'Father, into thy hands I commend my spirit.'
>>>>>> *S. Luke* xxiii. 46.

'Father'—last mortal speech of the immortal lips,
>> the speech of love, surrender, unity, and peace:
>> in one word expressing fullness of relationship
>> between God and man and thus of human
>>> brotherhood.
>> 'Father, hallowed be thy name, thy will be done.'

'Into thy hands'—the Son's obedience gathers the harvest of
>> all life;
>>> himself the vine, his blood the rising sap
>>>> to swell the vintage of the passing years:
>>> himself the fullness of all things created,
>>> Life and Light of men
>>>> dependent on the Father's will.

'I commend my spirit.'
>>> The Son of Man maintains the freedom of the human
>>>> choice,
>>>> in creaturely obedience to the end.
>>> The Son of God returns the love divine
>>>> that conquers death
>>>> and robs the grave of victory.
>>> Love dies the human death
>>>> that Love may raise humanity to God.

O Love, we praise and honour thee
for thy great love for us,
enduring to the end
that death might be the gate of life.

O Love, draw us so close to thee
through love's committal of ourselves
that when death comes to us
we shall remain with thee in life.

Lord, give me grace to follow thee and know thee,
the power of thy resurrection,
the fellowship of thy suffering,
conformed unto thy death.

XI

'And he bowed his head and gave up the ghost.'
S. Luke xxiii. 46.

My Love is crucified,
is made obedient unto death
with broken heart
and fallen head.
My Love is crucified,
is motionless in death.

The rest is silence
till the flesh assumes immortal shape,
the firstfruits from the tomb.

Immortal Saviour, Victor over death,
thyself the medicine of immortality,
by thy last breath we mortals pray
that when our bodies in the dust dissolve,
our spirits may abide secure with thee
till that great day when death shall be no more
and we shall see as we are seen:
draw thou our souls in life to thy obedience,
that ever looking to the end
we make each day of pilgrimage through time
a day whereby 'Our Father' may be for ever blessed:

may make each deed and thought
within the changing circumstance of mortal life
a bringing into being of thine accomplished kingdom,
the heavenly will made manifest:
preserve the souls that thou hast bought,
    that in the manifold temptations of this life
    they may through thee beat Satan down,
    delivered from the evil through thy grace.

          Thou callest.
              Needs must we come
          O loving Saviour to thy feet.

          Thou callest.
              Needs must we come
          O loving Saviour to thy feet:
              for thou art our God.

XII

'Lo, I am with you alway, even unto the end of the world. Amen.'
                              S. Matt. xxviii. 20.

My Lord and my God,
    the wounds are in thy feet, thy hands, thy brow,
    thy side is pierced,
    thy heart is broken for the sins of men.

          My Love is crucified.
              Hold thou me close
                  and closer to thy side
              that I, well-polished from the sins
                  of self-fullness may dwell in thee:
              that fear immoderate may pass
              and love which is not love for thee
                  in thee may die.

My Lord, my God,
    by thy Cross and Passion I appeal,
    by mark of nail and spear,
    by every scar upon thy brow,
    by every wound thou bore for men,
        give me thy love.

I

No love of mine can hold me to thy Cross:
  the things I would I do not,
  the things I loathe I do.
My life is sin; thy life is purity.

O Lord, forgive.
O Lord, lift up my heart to meet thy heart.
  No love of mine that springs from nature's source
    can be the love I hunger for;
  that love is all thy gift:
    it is thyself—
    thy love in me.

I cry to thee, forgive:
  a sinner in a world of sin
  that crucifies thy love.
I cry to thee, forgive:
  blind, maimed, and halt,
  in all my life corrupt
  in falling short of love.
I cry to thee, forgive:
  give me thy love,
  give me thyself,
  the very self thou gavest on the Cross for me,
  that I may give that love, thy love to thee.

    O heart of Jesus be my peace,
      thy wounded side my home,
      thy broken feet my following,
      thy pierced hands my guiding,
      thy crown of thorns my exceeding rich reward,
      thy Cross my daily toil,
      thy kiss the consummation of my bliss.

CHAPTER IX

AFFECTIVE REPETITION

I

'Thou art worthy, O Lord, to receive glory and honour and power: for thou hast created all things, and for thy pleasure they are and were created.'

Rev. iv. 11.

God,
> self-existing
> eternal
> Creator
> three persons one God
> Love:
>> I adore and praise thee.

God,
> one word, one syllable,
>> so insignificant within the utterance of mortal breath:
>> so weighty on the heart that holds the thought.

God,
> the sound passes, yet the thought remains
>> sustained and reinvigorated through the rhythm
>> of the speech whereby the word expressed maintains
>> the will's dependence, in creaturely response to
>>> the Unchangeable.

God,
> Almighty
> All-knowing
> supreme and infinite Good,
> Wisdom above all wisdom
> Life and Light of creatures,
>> I magnify and honour thee.

O God, my God,
>   all things speak of thee,
>   yet they are not thee.

O God, my God,
>   Almighty and Unchangeable,
>>   thou art present everywhere,
>>   whole everywhere
>>   without beginning and without end;
>   perfect Form and Beauty
>>   beyond all beauty of created form
>   thyself Form and Beauty self-existing,
>>   whereof creation is the mirror to reflect the Beautiful
>>   and is itself upheld and inseparably informed by
>>   thee, who madest it for thyself,
>>   who art my God.

O God,
>   it is enough for me to say again and yet again
>   this word descriptive of thyself, the Indescribable
>   wherein we live and move and have our being:
>   God, my God, my all, my life, my God.

God,
>   most Holy
>   most Just
>   most Merciful
>   most Intimate to those who love thee
>   most Compassionate to those who seek thee
>>   I thank and love thee.

O God, my God,
>   it is enough for me to make response
>>   in creaturely dependence,
>   to breathe the word descriptive of thy Infinite Perfection
>>   in rhythmic order, breath following breath,
>   to move my will to faith's assent
>>   so that the limited should answer to the Unlimited,
>>   and love should answer Love.

O God, my God,
>   thou madest me, thou sustainest me,
>   thou lovest me that I might love thee
>   in response and worship thee.

O God, my God,
>> make thou my heart and will to know
>>> that it is to thee it speaks:
>> person answering Person—'Yes.'

O God, my God,
>> thou art the Source and Being of my life;
>> for thee I am, to live with thee, and work for thee,
>> and worship thee in time and in eternity.

O God, my God,
>> in whom all life has life
>> through whom I am conjoined to all that lives;
>> it is in thee alone that I may find true peace
>> it is in thee alone all things are mine
>>> that life is mine, the angels are mine, the saints
>>> are mine, the righteous are mine and the sinners
>>>> are mine.

O God,
>> without thee, the earth is against me, the heaven
>>> against me,
>> the angels withstand me, the saints are separated from me,
>> the righteous are offended by me and injured by me,
>> the sinners are made more sinful by me.

O God,
>> without thee, in emptiness and fear I should exist,
>>> while death gnaws on me.

O God of mercy, God of grace,
>> teach me to hold myself so still,
>>> within the inmost centre of my soul,
>>> that I may know all things are thine,
>>> and none are mine unless thou givest me,
>>> that I and they may bless thy name.

O God of mercy, God of grace,
>> teach me to discipline my heart
>>> that every beat and pulse may witness give
>>> unto the life thou givest me, that I may live
>>> the bondslave of the liberating grace, one life

with thee unto the end of days, and endlessly
within the vision of the blest where thou
dost reign eternally.

O God of mercy, God of grace,
    teach me to hold my will attentive in the liberty
        thou gavest me,
      that I may will with thee to do thy will
        as thou dost show it me;
      draw me to respond to thee in each separate
      occasion of the passing time
      that when the vanities of earth
      are passed I may remain for ever
      in the loving rhythm of thy everlasting peace.

God,
    to be hallowed by all,
      our Father.
God,
    to be acknowledged by all,
      our Saviour.
God,
    to be accepted by all,
      our Sanctifier.
God,
    to be loved by all,
      most blessed Trinity.
God,
    that livest for ever and ever,
    to thee be glory, dominion, and power
    both now and ever.

O God of mercy, God of grace,
    have pity, spare and pardon,
    that I may never be separated from thee:
    when I fall away from thee in recollection,
      recall me,
    when I sin against thee,
      punish and restore me.
    Grant me perseverance to the end
      that in the hour of my death
      I may acknowledge thee,
             my God and my all.

II

'He that abideth in me, and I in him, the same bringeth forth much fruit; for without me ye can do nothing.'

S. John xv. 5.

Jesus,
      may I by repetition of thy Name
      be taught to hold myself so still,
      to lose myself in sacrificial discipline and prayer
      that nothing but thyself be all my doing.
Jesus,
      my life is short
      the years and moments are not mine to waste.
Jesus,
      my life restored
      is not mine own but purchased by thy Blood
      that I may use each opportunity of time
      to live for thee.
Jesus,
      master thou art to me,
      bondslave am I to thee.
Jesus,
      imprint thy Name upon my life
        that I may ever think and act
        not I but thee.
Jesus,
      may thy Name, thy holy Name
        so fill my heart and move my will
      that by the repetition of thy Name,
      Name most sweet, most wonderful
        before whose sound all things must bow,
      Name that is life and healing to the sick,
      Name that is freedom to the sinner's soul,
      Name exalted by the angel host,
      Name before which the devils tremble and depart,
      Name that is loved above all names by all the saints,
      Name that is thy Name, Jesus,
        my whole activity,
        my mind, my heart, my will be turned to thee,
               O Jesus.

Jesus,
>   thou only hast done everything for me:
>   What then must I give and do for thee?

Jesus,
>   it is I who must seek thee,
>   in humble penitence approaching thee.

Jesus,
>   it is I who must find thee
>   in the doing of thy will.

Jesus,
>   it is I who must knock and wait for thee
>   in loving confidence until thou openest to me.

Jesus,
>   it is I who must face the judgement,
>   when the books are opened
>   when every deed and thought are known;
>   the sinful years, the wasted moments,
>   the deeds undone, the sloth, the negligence.

Jesus,
>   I have no answer in thy judgement,
>   that others held me back from grosser sins,
>   that others helped me to be good by natural standards.

Jesus,
>   if I myself have not attained
>   then is the accusation written large,
>   for others' aid is opportunity to give and do the more.

Jesus,
>   he who buried his talent was condemned,
>   the negligent virgins were shut out,
>   and those who knew thee not
>   and served thee not in other folk were lost.

Jesus,
>   without thee I indeed am lost,
>   without thee sin doth hold me fast,
>   without thee I cannot act for thee to do thy will.

Jesus,
>   thou askest nothing but myself,
>   myself to love thee
>   my sins to forgive
>   my capacities to fulfil.

Jesus,
    thy love by deed was manifest,
    by Cross and Passion
    thou didst free me from the chain of sin
    that I, in thought and action, might return thy love.
Jesus,
    thou askest nothing but myself
        my doing of thy will.
Jesus,
    may I by repetition of thy Name
    always remember thee
        with my whole thinking, with desire and affection
        with all my imagination, with all my memory,
        understanding, reason, and attention.
Jesus,
    may I by repetition of thy Name
    perceive in every thought and opportunity to act
        an occasion and a way to love thee.
Jesus,
    when my feebleness has done its best,
        forgive where I have failed.
Jesus,
    mayest thou alone be praised
        for any good I do.

Jesus in the beginning
Jesus in the doing
Jesus in the end
    of every thinking, of every acting,
Jesus,
    if I remember thee
    then only can I act
        as thou wouldst have me act.
Jesus,
    then can I answer thee
        in faith, and hope, and charity.
Jesus,
    may I by repetition of thy Name
        be drawn to thee so close
        in worshipping response
        to hold thee still,

that I may know the living quiet of thy love,
the love that passeth understanding.

Jesus,

Beloved, thou art mine
and I am thine.
Thou standest at the lattice;
I sought thee and thou didst find me;
I lost thee and I seek thee
in the repetition of thy Name.

Jesus,

Beloved, I am thine
and thou art mine.
I lost thee and am found by thee
in the repetition of thy Name.
Thou standest at the door;
my heart is moved in quick response
by repetition of thy Name,
I found thee and yet I lost thee.

Jesus,

where dwellest thou?
I seek thee in the repetition of thy Name.

Jesus,

Beloved, amongst the lilies
thy flock thou feedest
in the garden of surrender and obedience to thy will.

Jesus,

may I be swift and patient
to follow thee, stripped of all save love
to be found of thee and hold thee
in the repetition of thy Name.

Jesus,

draw me to thyself
in meek obedience,
in loss of sensible desire whereby I claim
'Thou art mine':
in loss of conscious possessiveness whereby I assert
'I am thine':
in gain of humble submissiveness
leaving all to thee, whereby I say
'I am my Beloved's'
the bondslave of my Lord:

      'Thy desire is toward me'
    not my will but thine be done.
Jesus,
      Beloved, I am thine.
      Thy desire is toward me,
      my love is thine
        because thou first didst love me.
Jesus,
      thou art the Bridge
      restoring man to God.
Jesus,
      awake my soul by repetition of thy Name
      to penitence, that I may seek.
Jesus,
      the sinner falls before thy feet:
      O Lord forgive that I may enter on thy way.
Jesus,
      thy love lifts up the faltering soul
      in knowledge of redemptive care.
Jesus,
      awake my soul, by repetition of thy Name,
      to labour diligently in dying to myself,
        that I may find thy life in me.
Jesus,
      thy heart imparts the life that conquers sin.
      O Lord give strength that I may live.
Jesus,
      thy kiss is knowledge of eternity
      to those the few who reach in life unto that blessedness.
Jesus,
      awake thou my soul, by repetition of thy Name,
      that I may knock
      nor cease from knocking
        when all the feeling of this life is dry.
Jesus,
      hold fast my soul to watch and pray
      lest in the darkness I should fail thee.
Jesus,
      may the sweetness of thy Name repeated
      content my empty soul
        that I may knock

in faith upheld,
in hope expectant,
in charity expressed,
to wait thy will.

Jesus,
no act of mine may reach thy lips;
'Seek, find, and knock' is all my part;
'It shall be opened' is thy gift.

Jesus,
thy love all fear dispelleth.
Why should I fear
as if thou wouldst forget me?
Perfect my love
that it may cast out fear.

Jesus,
the sins of men cry out for judgement;
thou sufferest its pain
that love may rule where sin did reign.

Jesus,
I praise thee, the victory over sin and death is thine,
I desire no glory in the battle
for I am nothing worth.
Hold thou me close to purge my sin
and make me thine.

Jesus,
I praise thee, for the victory is thine.
Extend thy sufferings in me
that I may know thy victory—
may rejoice in thee, with thee,
my Jesus.

Jesus,
may thy Name repeated
be all my doing
Jesus, my Jesus,
Jesus, Jesus.

Jesus,
may I by repetition of thy Name
so wholly rest in thee
in silence held
in the deep quietude of self-forgetfulness
uninterrupted by successive thought

except the rhythm of my praise and adoration
    of thy loveliness
that I may be upheld in thee in unity of will
held fast by thee
    and holding thee
    a branch within the vine
    to bear thy fruit
    and rest in thee
             my Jesus.

Jesus,
    may I by repetition of thy Name,
      made one with thee,
    be offered in thy Love
    unto the Father's Love,
    one with the Holy Spirit's Love
      within the Blessed Trinity.

III

'*Having therefore, brethren, boldness to enter into the holiest by the blood of Jesus.*'

                                        Heb. x. 19.

Blood shed for many
Blood life-giving stream
Blood shed for remission of sins
Blood encompassing all life
Blood destroying death
Blood overcoming him who had the power of death
Blood by which Michael was victorious
Blood liberating all from Satan's power:
Blood of Jesus,
    sap of the vine
    river of life
    upwelling in every faithful heart:
Blood of Jesus,
    sustaining the soul in darkness
    refreshing the soul in light
    source of the victories of the saints:
Blood of the Lamb, slain from the foundation of the world
    the same, yesterday, to-day, and forever,

whom the angels, dominations, and powers
    praise and fear,
whom the heavens, cherubim, and seraphim exalt,
whom the Church acclaims
    with ceaseless adoration:
Blood of the Lamb
    that pleads for sinners in the heavenly places,
    one sacrifice, complete:
Blood of the Lamb
    on earth the sinner's food:
Blood one and the same for all:
Blood that never changes.
    Lord by thy Blood we pray—
    Unite thy Church on earth and make us one.

IV

'God is love; and he that dwelleth in love dwelleth in God, and God in him.'

1 S. John iv. 16.

Love is the new commandment of the Lord of Life,
    that man restored in him
    should love as he doth love.
Love fulfils and is the life
    that loses self through sacrifice.
Love forms the human personality
    through loss of separateness,
    whereby the individuality of self is clothed upon,
    transformed from death to life.
Love is creative,
    whereby I live,
    not I but Christ in me.
Love is redemptive,
    whereby the dead in sin
    are raised together alive in Christ
    that they may sit together in Christ Jesus
    in the heavenly place
    eternally at one.
Love uniteth all in love,
    each separate life made one

as leaves within one book
 the book of life
· as separate flames of sanctity
 one fire, Love's burning Light.
Love is God's very love most rich in mercy
 wherein he loved us,
 that man in Christ restored
 might be the praise of Glory
 and love return.
Love giveth life
 wherein the self becomes
 the ground and temple of the Paraclete,
 that man might sing and do and be the praise of God,
 in love established.
Love is the crown and end of life
 the conqueror of death,
 for without love both faith and hope must fail;
 for without love the devils fear and tremble
 and without love the heart grows sick
 with hope deferred.
 Love, only love, can cast out fear.
 Love, only love, can conquer doubt.
Love is itself, the witness of itself
 in action proved
 by knowledge of itself in Love's exchange
 in liberty of will, love given freely in love's return of love.
Love is itself complete within itself
 fulfilling all, completing all
 that life can give and be.
Love is not passion,
 wherein the tension of self-full excitement
 seeks release in temporary appeasement,
 seeking the satisfaction of completeness
 because it feels its incompleteness,
 yet never finding resting-place within
 the temporal changes of mortality.
Love is not fellowship,
 wherein a common interest
 overcomes and orders selfishness to social ends,
 in co-operation of mutual gain
 and satisfaction of a common purpose.

Love is itself the witness of itself,
    the ray proceeding from the uncreated heart of Love
    that binds the creature to its Love,
    whereby the certainty of Love is proved
        in superexcellence of knowing—
        knowledge beyond all knowledge of times
            and circumstances,
    wherein the burden of succession falls away
        and love held in stillness to Love
            is Love's reality.
Love is itself its own fulfilment
    within the flow and rhythm of itself
    beyond all time and difference of occasion
    complete
    love answering Love
    for Love is love's beginning
    it has no end.
            O Love, I am content
            hold thou me still.

Love is the giving of the self in service:
Love is the finding of the self in other's needs:
Love is the fulfilment of the self in being love,
    wherein sufficiency of self
        gives place to worship in dependence and humility:
    wherein the separateness finds completion
        in acknowledgement and restoration
            of creation's oneness:
    wherein each gives and serves each other:
    wherein the common whole of life revolves
        in harmony of giving and return,
        diversity in unity,
        in purpose one,
        to glorify the perfect Unity of Trinity.
Love quickens love to answer love's desire
    is perfected in patient holding-on to Love
    is purged in suffering in the temporal,
        on grace dependent
        overcoming sin
    is proved, expectant, prostrate

at the threshold of the door of Love
    empty of all save love
    content to knock and knock untiringly
    because such is the will of God;
    assured in confidence,
    content because the darkness is not lovelessness
    but blind assent
      to Love himself
    whereby love waits on Love
      as long as Love shall will
      and as Love wills.

        O Love, I am content
          hold thou me still.
Love is the point wherein all creatures meet and rest,
    possessing and possessed
    within the heart of Love.
Love is the still point within creation's measured dance
    motionless in all but love's own movement
    acquiescent in dependence
    responsive unto the touch of Love
    whereby the creature
      unmoved, unstirred,
      uninterrupted by the vanities that pass
      unresponsive to the pulse of time
    is held attentive to the Limitless
      knowing in one moment all moments
      within the flow and reflow of Love's immediateness,
          the Sea pacific.

        O Love, I am content
          hold thou me still that I may know
          the heart and pulse and movement of Love.

Love is the completion and fullness of itself
      within the Unity of Trinity alone,
    wherein the Love of Father is outpoured
    in limitless activity unto the Son,
    wherein the Love of Son is to the Father turned

K

wherein the Love, Love of the Father and of the Son
is Love himself, the Holy Paraclete
proceeding from the Father and the Son.

LOVE, THREE PERSONS, EACH LOVE
PERFECT AND COMPLETE IN ONE LOVE,
COMBINED AND INTIMATELY RELATED,
FOR LOVE IS GIVING AND EXCHANGE OF LOVE
IN PERFECT UNITY.

NOTES

CHAPTER I

p. 26, l. 13, *visible 'becoming'*

cf. Romans i. 20, 'For the invisible things of him from the creation of the world are clearly seen, being understood through the things that are made.'

p. 27, l. 17, *stuttering will*

I owe this most effective and descriptive phrase to the Rev. Austin Farrer's book, *Finite and Infinite*, p. 113.

p. 28, ll. 20 ff., *memory, understanding, will*

The three powers of the soul. For their use in meditation see the first exercise in S. Ignatius' *Spiritual Exercises*, and for commentary, the edition of Father Longridge, S.S.J.E., particularly his note C, p. 208, and quotation from Father Benson, S.S.J.E., on use of understanding and affections: 'The understanding does but supply the data upon which the affections are to act. Every effort therefore of the understanding, whatever its result may be, should lead us to love . . .,' (p. 210).

p. 29, l. 3 *whose prayer*

cf. S. John xvii.

p. 29, l. 37, *that I may know myself*

The work of self-knowledge is particularly that of mortification, whereby the will may be freed from the idols of sinful desire and directed towards righteousness.

p. 33, l. 13, *coinherence*

cf. S. John xv. 4. Charles Williams, in his study of the Holy Spirit, *The Descent of the Dove* (Faber, 1939), uses this idea freely, as for example on p. 10:

'The new state of being, a state of redemption, of co-inherence, made actual by that Divine substitution, "He in us and we in Him." '

CHAPTER II

The foundation of this chapter is a booklet of the same title, first published in 1924 by the Society of SS. Peter and Paul with a preface by the Rev. W. B. Trevelyan. The Church Literature Association who took over the booklet from the original publishers have given their permission for its rearrangement and incorporation in this collection. The devotions were gathered for the most part from Bishop Andrewes' *Preces Privatae*, Blosius' *Spiritual Exercises*, and Arvisenet's *Solemn Warnings*; a few were from other sources or original. The whole has been reordered and new matter added for the present book.

I have included in this chapter a few well-known prayers which are specially suitable for use by the second method of S. Ignatius; that is, the slow recitation of the prayer, holding each line or phrase as long as the attention can find suitable occupation.

S. Ignatius suggests that the user should say a word or phrase and (1) 'dwell on the consideration of this word so long as he finds meanings, comparisons, relish and consolation in thoughts pertaining to it; and let him act in the same way with regard to each word of the *Our Father*, or [any word or phrase] of any other prayer whatsoever that he shall wish to pray in this manner.'

(2) If the one word or phrase occupies the whole hour or time set aside for prayer he should not leave the subject being prayed on but conclude at the end of the time with a quick vocal recitation of the rest of the prayer.

(3) It is profitable to continue with the same prayer till it is thoroughly worked over, so the next prayer time should be given to the next word or phrase, beginning the prayer with the simple vocal expression of what has already been done.

Finally S. Ignatius reminds us that the proper conclusion to such a prayer is a short practical colloquy:

'he should turn himself to the Person to whom the prayer was directed, and in a few words ask for the virtues or graces which he feels himself more especially to need.'

p. 36, l. 1, *Remember . . .*

S. Francis of Assisi at the Chapter of the Rush-mats:

' "My little children, great things have we promised unto God, much greater far hath God promised unto us, if we observe what we have promised unto Him; and of a surety shall we behold what hath been promised to us. Short-lived is the joy of the world; the pain that follows it is everlasting; little are the pains of this life, but the glory of the other life is infinite." And on these words, preaching most devoutly, he comforted the brothers, and turned their hearts into obedience and reverence. . . .'—*Little Flowers of S. Francis*, Chap. xviii.

p. 36, l. 18, *Take . . .*

'More even than the Anima Christi, of which he is not the author, this is S. Ignatius' prayer.'—Joseph Rickaby, *S.J.*, *The Spiritual Exercises*, p. 211.

The prayer is frequently used and if separated from its context in the Ignatian Exercises (where it appears in 'the Contemplation for obtaining love') its full significance and deeper meanings can easily be lost. The devout soul should study its setting in the Exercises, and particularly the commentary provided by Father Longridge, S.S.J.E., in his translation of *The Spiritual Exercises of S. Ignatius Loyola* (Mowbrays), in which he points out that the prayer is 'an heroic act of resignation . . . the greatest surely and the most heroic that can be conceived' (p. 156).

p. 37, ll. 10 f., *Christ be with me . . .*

An arrangement of the essential elements of the Christocentric portion of the prayer of S. Patrick, known as the 'Breastplate.' In this order, as I have set it out, the soul will find himself making the sign of the Cross and binding himself in it, from every assault of man or fiend and from every direction, as he invokes Christ's protection and prays for union with his Lord.

As a matter of interest, a literal translation from the old Irish, quoted from the *Catholic Encyclopaedia*, is as follows:

> 'Christ protect me to-day
> > against every poison, against burning
> > against drowning, against death-wound
> > that I may receive abundant reward.
> Christ with me, Christ before me
> Christ behind me, Christ within me
> Christ beneath me, Christ above me
> Christ at my right, Christ at my left
> Christ in the fort
> Christ in the chariot seat
> Christ in the poop
> Christ in the heart of every one that thinks of me
> Christ in the mouth of every one who speaks to me
> Christ in every eye that sees me
> Christ in every ear that hears me.'

The whole prayer reflects the dangers and journeys of the missionary age. Another adaptation drawn from Bishop Andrewes appears on p. 47 and a portion on p. 49. Repetition, when the context is suitable, is an aid to devotion.

p. 41, l. 28, *Thank*

cf. Julian of Norwich, *The Revelations of Divine Love* (edited by Grace Warrack. Methuen):

'And also to prayer belongeth thanking. Thanking is a true inward knowing, with great reverence and lovely dread turning ourselves with all our mights unto the working that our good Lord stirreth us to. . . . And sometime when the heart is dry and feeleth not, or else by temptation of our enemy—then it is driven by reason and by grace to cry upon our Lord with voice, rehearsing his blessed Passion and his great Goodness; and the virtue of our Lord's word turneth into the soul and quickeneth the heart and entereth [i.e. leadeth] it by his grace into true working, and maketh it pray right blissfully' (Chap. xli).

p. 44, l. 32, *I am naught.* cf. Note on Chap. v.

p. 45, l. 38, *prevent.*

The reader may need reminding that owing to the change in the meaning of words through the course of time, this does not mean *hinder* the future but *go before* the future, as in the Prayer Book collects: 'thy grace may always prevent and follow us' (Trinity xvii) and 'Prevent us, O Lord, in all our doings . . . begun, continued, and ended in thee.'

p. 47, ll. 17 ff., *Lord Jesus*
Devout petitions of S. Augustine.

p. 49, l. 15, *Abyss*
There are those who will criticize the use of words such as this in devotion on the ground that they may become meaningless abstractions, or that they may lead to quietist, or even theosophical, ideas of the loss of the soul's

identity in Deity. However that may be (and the devout soul must be careful in the use of words) I do not know any other word which conveys sufficiently vividly the idea of the unlimitedness and boundlessness of the Divine life. S. Catherine of Siena in her *Dialogue* makes use of the term 'for I have tasted and seen into the light of the intellect in thy light, the abyss of thee'; and again, 'Oh! Abyss, oh! Eternal Godhead, oh! sea profound' (translation by Algar Thorold, Kegan Paul, 1907, p. 332).

The Divine sea and the soul as a fish is a classical concept of mystical writers, for it preserves the distinction between the soul and the Creator. The soul is in God, possessed by God and possessing God, but without identification or loss of identity in God, for such would negative and over-throw the nature and purpose of the creature, which is the worship and love of God.

p. 50, l. 1, *Would it were kindled*

S. Luke xii. 49. Moffatt and others translate thus, preserving the sense of the parallel in *v.* 50.

CHAPTER III

Most of the matter in this chapter appeared originally in the Burgh Booklet series as *A Pilgrim's Chapbook.*

pp. 54, 57, 58, *Worship, thanksgiving, and intercession*

The practice of prayer has sometimes been divided for the purpose of discussion into the several activities of worship, thanksgiving, and inter-cession. Prayer is not a technique in which each separate part can be isolated like a piece of machinery and defined separately as a self-sufficient whole. It is a living operation—the filial response of the creature to the Creator. Therefore, though this chapter makes use of these divisions, prefaced by the fallen creature's need of conducting all prayer in penitence, it does not imply that the divisions are to be considered as mutually exclu-sive. Each division must pass into the others and be supported by the others. Worship robbed of thanksgiving can easily become a barren and formal exercise. Thanksgiving is cold and selfish if it lacks worship. Inter-cession becomes cramped and lifeless without the other two.

The division is convenient as it illustrates three primary aspects of the response by the soul, possessing intelligence and free will, to its Creator:

(i) The offering by the soul of itself—the sum total of its creaturely life —to its Source and End, and in this offering the loving regard of the creature to its Creator by whose love it is enabled to love and to offer itself. Worship is essentially an acted dependence. This dependence may be variously expressed as praise and as adoration.

(ii) The rational appreciation of the Creator and the goodness of his operations. The first may be described as blessing and magnification; the second as gratitude.

(iii) The submission of the created liberty to be 'one with the energy' of the Creator. Regarding God's gifts of grace, we supplicate his assis-tance; regarding the needs of creation, including ourselves, we hold them to God in intercession.

p. 52, ll. 10 ff., *Praise, reverence, service*

cf. Principles and Foundation of the Ignatian Exercises. For commentary, see p. 26 et seq. of *The Spiritual Exercises of S. Ignatius of Loyola*, Father W. H. Longridge, S.S.J.E.

p. 59, l. 1, *nothing of myself*

For an expansion of this thought cf. *Cambridge Bede Book*, No. lxvi, Rev. E. Milner-White, O.G.S. (1936):
'Blessed Jesu, lifting up holy hands perpetually for all mankind: breathe by thy spirit such love into the prayers I offer, that they may be taken into thine, and prevail with thine.'

p. 60, l. 1, *the ground of all beseeching*

cf. Julian of Norwich, *Revelations of Divine Love*, Chap. xli.
'And all this brought our Lord suddenly to my mind, and shewed these words and said: I am the ground of thy beseeching: first it is my will that thou have it; and after I make thee to will it; and after I make thee to beseech it and thou beseechest it. How then should it then be that thou shouldest not have thy beseeching?'

CHAPTER IV

The Psalter is a storehouse of phrases for affective prayer. The regular recitation of the Office leads naturally to the memorizing and use of phrases which have struck the attention or met some passing need of the soul.

It is a good exercise to work over the Psalter and pick out a selection of passages which can be used for vocal aspirations. This chapter is intended to serve as an example. The selected phrases are here collected in a series of separate devotions. Each section has its own central theme illustrated by a quotation from the *Imitation*. They are best used by carefully thinking over the quotation as a preparation, before beginning the section. The phrases should then be repeated slowly and the mind should be allowed to rest on each phrase as long as the attention will remain fixed. If the mind begins to wander, or distractions surge in, the phrase can be repeated again and again until the need of a renewal of thought makes it necessary to pass on to the next phrase, when the same repetition can be carried on with that phrase, and so on until the end of the section. A conclusion could be made by returning to the first phrase which sets the subject or theme, or by gathering the devotion together and offering it in the prayer set out at the end of the last section. cf. Note on Chap. ii, p. 36, l. 18, on the second Ignatian method.

p. 61, l. 9, *Righteousness*

Righteousness is an attribute of Deity, which his creatures must manifest. It is connected with the idea of order, and should be differentiated from the conception of holiness, which is the expression of the unity of the creaturely life with God. The two conceptions are intimately related, for unless we do right we cannot be holy. and unless we are growing in holiness we cannot do right.

p. 62, l. 23, *Poor* . . .

It should be remembered that 'poor' in the Bible has got a much wider meaning than it has to-day. Apart from its customary meaning of material necessity, or of lack of any influence, it implies an awareness of spiritual need, and a willing reliance on the grace of God, which our Lord described as a 'blessed' state. In Revelation iii. 17 there is the further sense of poverty caused by the lack of this awareness and reliance on God.

In the same clause 'for the comfortless trouble's sake' has lost its meaning. Moffatt renders the verse (*Ps.* xii. 5):

'The weak are being crushed, the needy sigh; so I take action, says the Eternal One, and set them safe where they long to be.'

CHAPTER V

This chapter was originally *Prayers for the Quiet Hour*, Series I and II (Burgh Booklets, 3 and 4).

p. 69, l. 32, *I am nothing*

cf. 'I am naught; I have naught; naught I seek nor covet but the love of Jesus.'—Walter Hilton, *The Scale of Perfection* (Burns, Oates: Orchard Series, No. 13, 1927). cf. also Chap. ii, p. 44, l. 32.

CHAPTER VI

The devotions of this chapter were originally published in the Burgh Booklet series (No. 5) as *A Pilgrim's Chapbook*, Part II.

p. 77, l. 14, *silence*

Silence is too often thought of as being only a negative abstraction descriptive of an absence of noise. On the contrary it should be understood to be a positive means, in and through which the soul may come to a knowledge of spiritual reality.

p. 78, l. 2, *enslave*

cf. Romans vi. 22: 'δουλωθέντες δὲ τῷ Θεῷ' which looks back to *v.* 6: 'that we be no longer slaves [δουλεύειν] to sin.' The word 'enslave' may be strong for modern taste, which tends to think in terms of service as a contract entered upon and determinable by the choice of the parties concerned and not as one of status, wherein the servant is bound by duty to his lord, and which is determinable only by capture by a stronger master, or by the deliberate and successful desertion of the servant. There can be no question of contract between Creator and creature. Man owes a duty of service because he is created, though he also possesses (as a gift of God, not of his own merit) the capacity to appreciate and be attracted towards his true end. He is held by a double cord of duty and attraction. The emphasis will vary in practice between the two; the difficulty of their reconciliation is well discussed by Austin Farrer, *Finite and Infinite*, pp. 153, 154.

p. 82, l. 19, *myself all naked*

cf. *Imitation*, Book III, Chap. xxxvii. 3.

> 'ut ab omni proprietate possis expoliari
> et nudus nudum Jesum sequi;
> tibi mori: et mihi aeternitaliter vivere.'

p. 82, l. 29, *making many rich*

It is interesting to recall that S. Gilbert of Sempringham in his last words offered his life to his Lord in recalling His beneficence: 'He hath dispersed abroad and given to the poor; yes, he hath dispersed to many persons, he gave, he did not sell; it was to the poor, too, not to the rich.'

p. 85, l. 27, *to possess love alone*

This is well expressed by George Macdonald, *Diary of an Old Soul*: 'So to love perfectly, love perfect Love, love thee.'

p. 89, l. 30, *be agonized . . .*

cf. Pascal, *Pensées:* 'Jesus will suffer to the end of the world, and meantime we may not sleep,' and 'It seems to me that Jesus Christ, after his resurrection, allows only his wounds to be touched—"noli me tangere." We must be united only to his sufferings' (trans. G. B. Rawlings, publ. Scott. Sects. cxxxvi, cxxxix).

CHAPTER VII

This chapter originally appeared in the Burgh Booklet series. It has been pruned into shape as a meditation with considerations, a composition of place, four points, and a resolution, with the prayers as colloquies.

p. 92, l. 18, *O Mystery of Love*

cf. Catherine of Siena, *Dialogue*, p. 91:
'O Loving Madman! was it not enough for thee to become incarnate, that thou must also die?'

p. 96, l. 16, *bears the living Lord*

A parallel thought, expressed by Alcuin (735-804), is translated by Miss Helen Waddell as:

> 'Here, dying on the cross, the world's life hung,
>   Laving a world's sin in that deathly tide.
> That down-bent head raised earth above the stars.
>   O timeless wonder, life, because One died.'

p. 100, l. 10, *in will and signified by deed*:

cf. Richard Rolle, *The Form of Living*, Chap. iv:
'No thing that I do without proves that I love God; for a wicked man might do as much penance in body, as much waking and fasting as I do. How may I then ween that I love, or hold myself better for that any man may do? Certes, whether my heart loves God or not wots none but God, for aught that they may see me do. Wherefore love is verily in will, not in work save as a sign of love. For he that says he loves God, and will not do in act what is in him to show love, tell him that he lies.'

CHAPTER VIII

A small portion of this chapter appeared as additional matter to bind together translations of sections of the early English treatise *A Talkynge of the Love of God*, published as *Prayers and Meditations for the Lovers of Jesus*.

p. 106, l. 34, *mode*

cf. 'for the ordinances of Holy Church rest in rule and mode, and weight and measure.'—*The Book of the Twelve Béguines*, Chap. v.

Mode and *modeless* are translations of Ruysbroek's 'wise' and 'no wise' expressing the contrast between the ordered rational cognizance of the temporal and the intuitive altogether appreciation of the immediateness of the spiritual.

p. 107, l. 8, *we must not sleep*

See note on Chapter vi (*be agonized*), p. 89, l. 30.

p. 116, l. 7, *no longer pertinent*

Taken as a whole there is much that could be found alike in the present situation and in that figured by Piers Plowman, except it is not the worldly priest but the complacency of ordinary Church folk whom 'this folk hath enchanted, and plastered them so pleasantly they dread no sin' (*The Vision of Antichrist*).

p. 119, l. 32, *bridge*

The image is drawn from that in the *Dialogue* of S. Catherine of Siena: 'And so, wishing to remedy your great evils, I have given you the Bridge of my Son, in order that, passing across the flood, you may not be drowned, which flood is the tempestuous sea of this dark life. See, therefore, under what obligations the creature is to me, and how ignorant he is, not to take the remedy which I have offered, but to be willing to drown' (p. 74).

p. 120, l. 2, *gate of penitence*

The bridge has three steps. The first is of our Lord's feet, the second his wounded side wherein he 'manifesteth the secret of his heart, the third his lips where the soul finds peace from the terrible war she has been waging with her sin.'

'On the first step, lifting her feet from the affections of the earth, the soul strips herself of vice; on the second she fills herself with love and virtue; and on the third she tastes peace' (p. 78).

p. 122, l. 12, *licentiously* is here used in its strict meaning—the opposite of ordered obedience, with all the evil that flows from such licence.

p. 124, l. 36, *discipleship*

It should be noted that the Gospel command is 'Go make disciples'; there is nothing said about adherents. It is obvious that through what Toynbee (cf. vol. i, *A Study of History*, p. 191) calls *mimésis*, adherency is bound to arise, and that the tendency will be, as it has been, for the Church to organize herself in the world to preserve the conformity of an adherency rather than encouraging a discipleship. The fluctuating balance of this process is well described by Bishop Kirk in *The Vision of God* (Longmans, 1931).

Adherency must grow into discipleship, yet wherever adherency outweighs discipleship the Church is weak and tends to be Laodicean. Revival can only come by an increase of discipleship. If we are to look for a new revival of Christian power in these days it can only come by the renewing of an apostolate ready to buy up the opportunities through prayer and sacrifice.

p. 127, l. 25, *fear immoderate*

cf. *Imitation*, Book III, Chap. xxxvii:

'Then shall all vain imaginations, evil disturbances,
    and superfluous cares cease (*or* fade away).
Then shall immoderate fear withdraw,
    and affection that is out of order die.'

p. 128, l. 30, *thy kiss* (see also p. 137, l. 28).

This line, to follow the imagery of S. Catherine, refers to the third and highest step of the bridge, and is proper rather to the unitive prayer life than to the illuminative; and to contemplative prayer rather than affective. It is, however, the proper and fitting completion of this prayer if it is prayed with understanding and humility, for it expresses the truth about our life of devotion which can be completed only in the conscious union with the Beloved either here or in the life beyond the gate of death.

The experimental knowledge of God, which is infused contemplation, is not secured by desire: in fact desire or passion of ill-ordered devotion may hinder it, if it be God's will to bestow it. We can only prepare for it and co-operate with it by self-stripping and with increasing penitence and a sorrow for sin, both personal and corporate, and wait in patience 'knocking' till 'it shall be opened.'

If it should be given, for it is the gift of God, it does not mean the end of suffering but rather the purification of suffering, so that the soul may know and experience the sharing and overcoming of suffering in the victory of creative Love.

The use of this expression is justified by the tradition of Christian devotional writers, but it must be strictly construed to mean what they mean. It is a dangerous phrase for the unmortified, for it signifies the union of the soul to its Lord and Saviour—a union made by the act of God, not through the desire of the soul; and in surrender of will and not through fervent emotion. Yet the prayer would be incomplete if the reasonable desire of the soul for its completeness were not mentioned. The phrase should not be used by those who do not understand what it means in discipline of self, and in waiting in humility and patience at the door of his love.

CHAPTER IX

This chapter is entitled 'Affective Repetitions' to distinguish the method of letting the intelligence and affections fill out the meaning of the simple repetition of the one word, from that of a bare mechanical repetition which is more of the nature of a *mantra* than a prayer. Irrational repetition is always dangerous, especially if the emotions are being forced by the repetition in order to arrive at a self-induced and fallacious unification of the attention.

p. 129, l. 9, *one word*

cf. S. Augustine:

'So then, those words which are spoken, and pass away, are sounds, are letters, are syllables. The word which sounds passes away, but that which the sound signified, which was within the speaker, as he thought thereon, and within the hearer, while apprehending it, the word remains still, when the sounds have passed away' (*Homilies on S. John i. 8*, trans. 'Library of Fathers').

p. 130, l. 9, *beauty*

cf. *Dionysius on the Divine Names*; trans. C. E. Rolt (S.P.C.K., p. 95):

'Now there is a distinction between the titles "Beautiful" and "Beauty" applied to the all-embracing Cause. For we universally distinguish these two titles, as meaning respectively the qualities shared, and the objects that share therein. We give the name Beautiful to that which shares in the quality of beauty, and we give the name Beauty to that common quality by which all beautiful things are beautiful.

'But the super-essential Beauty is called "Beauty" because of that quality which It imparts to all things severally according to their nature, and because It is the Cause of the harmony and splendour in all things, flashing forth upon them like light, the beautifying communications of Its originating ray: . . . And it is called "Beautiful" because It is All-Beautiful and more than Beautiful, and is eternally, unvaryingly, unchangeably Beautiful. . . . It contains in a transcendent manner the originating beauty of everything that is beautiful.'

Rolt comments: 'The true beauty of all beautiful things is outside them in God. Hence all great art (even when not directly religious) tends towards the Supernatural or has a kind of supernatural atmosphere' (p. 96).

p. 131, l. 14, *the angels are mine . . .*

cf. S. John of the Cross, *Spiritual Sentences and Maxims* (Allison Peers' translation), vol. iii, p. 244:

'Mine are the heavens and mine is the earth; mine are the people, the righteous are mine and mine are the sinners; the angels are mine and the Mother of God, and all things are mine; and God Himself is mine and for me, for Christ is mine and all for me. What, then, dost thou ask for and seek, my soul? Thine is all this, and it is all for thee."

p. 133, l. 4, *sacrificial discipline and prayer*

cf. S. Peter of Alcantara, *A Golden Treatise of Mental Prayer* (edit. G. S. Hollings, S.S.J.E., p. 179):

'So that, neither is work of benefit to us, without prayer, nor is prayer without work, because it is not lasting, because it will not bear fruit. But with these two powers we shall be God's living Temple with its two departments, one of Sacrifice, and one of Prayer.'

p. 134, l. 5, *'it is I who must seek thee . . . it is I who must find thee'*

This figure of 'seeking' and 'finding' Jesus, together with the thought of his own command 'Abide in me and I in you,' is well treated by Walter Hilton, *The Scale of Perfection*, especially Book I, Chaps. xlvi-xlix. He advocates the method we have called 'Affective Repetition.' 'He is in thy soul, and never shall be lost out of it. Nevertheless, thou art never the